# Principles *of* Leadership

Secular and Theological Principles
That Define Success and Growth

## TROY P. ZEHNDER

WESTBOW
P R E S S®
A DIVISION OF THOMAS NELSON
& ZONDERVAN

Scripture taken from the New King James Version. Copyright © 1979, 1980, 1982 by Thomas Nelson, Inc. Used by permission. All rights reserved.

WestBow Press books may be ordered through booksellers or by contacting:

WestBow Press
A Division of Thomas Nelson & Zondervan
1663 Liberty Drive
Bloomington, IN 47403
www.westbowpress.com
1 (866) 928-1240

ISBN: 978-1-5127-3474-4 (sc)
ISBN: 978-1-5127-3475-1 (e)

Print information available on the last page.

WestBow Press rev. date: 06/15/2016

# CONTENTS

# INTRODUCTION

Secular and theological principles that define success and growth are the same principles with different applications. In fact, when it comes to leadership, the same qualities apply to practically every situation. The application may vary depending on the circumstances of the job involved, but the fundamental elements remain the same. Whether you are leading a family, a school function, a board meeting, or troops, at some point in time you will be looked to for guidance, and the way you respond will determine the flow of events that dramatically impact the future.

Throughout the course of this book, principles will be evaluated from the secular perspective to build dynamic units. Whether those units are small businesses, large companies, or families, the simple application of a few short principles can make the difference between success and failure. The theological perspective is geared more toward the religious lives of everyone. Examples of perfect leadership are prevalent all throughout scripture, and the application of these examples in the modern life can create a life-changing experience.

Type the word "leadership" into a search engine, and endless pages will appear which are devoted to various professions. The concept of leadership is not difficult to find; however, it is easily misunderstood. To many people, "leadership" is a term they do not aspire to embrace, because they do not believe they are in a position to lead. That is an unfortunate misunderstanding, as all people at one time or another in life will be in a position of leadership whether they recognize it or not.

# LEADERSHIP AND MANAGEMENT ARE NOT SYNONYMOUS

*Secular Significance*

There is a common misperception, particularly in the business world, that being a manager and being a leader are identical roles. This belief could not be further from the truth. While it is true that good leaders possess the ability to be, and in fact often are, good managers, simply being a manager does not make one a good leader. One factor at play in this misperception is simply not understanding the terminology and applying it in an accurate manner.

"Management" is a basic term for maintaining the status quo within a set of given parameters. A term that is synonymous with "management" is "governance." Whether or not governing is carried out by a political body—such as the federal, state, or local government—there is a set of parameters that clearly define the boundaries that the particular body must operate in. Throughout the multitude of truck stops and diners in our nation, one commonly hears the expression that the country "lacks effective leadership." While that statement is true, a more accurate statement to begin with would be to declare that our country "lacks effective management."

The Constitution of the United States clearly lays out boundaries in which the federal government is allowed to operate. However, these boundaries are regularly pushed aside and deemed too outdated and old-fashioned to be of significance today. If that is the case, then

1

government takes on an entirely different meaning, as no parameters exist in which elected officials are held to manage. When parameters are radically changed or disappear from management, chaos ensues. That is certainly evident in our government today.

In the case of constitutions, whether they are federal, state, or local, the ability exists to make alterations to them in order that they may function in a more effective manner. When these changes are made in an effort to produce positive results, it can be said that our officials displayed good leadership. When these same efforts produce poor results, the decisions are recognized as a lack of leadership. Does this truly qualify as leadership though? In order to make changes, there are still parameters that must be adhered to. For this to truly be leadership, participants must stretch the boundaries in front of them to allow for change. This simply does not exist in areas defined by constitutions. As a whole, leadership in this arena still serves a significant purpose, but it does so within the context of the principles an individual possesses—not within the result of legislation.

There is a difference in types of parameters between governments and businesses, as government parameters are in essence laws, which are rigid and difficult to change for a reason. In business, parameters need to be flexible in order for a business to grow and accomplish a goal. This same style of parameters exists in military operations in which flexibility is the key to achieving an objective and the leadership of a unit must be relied on to function effectively. So how does leadership now apply to management?

Leaders possess the ability to stretch parameters in order to generate growth, cohesion, and the effectiveness of the unit they are charged with. This is a quality that should spur growth and achievement. But notice that the parameters are not radically changed; they are merely expanded. A good leader operates with an ability to push his people to do better than the status quo, within the flexible parameters. This obviously cannot apply to elected officials, who are tasked with obeying laws and operating strictly within their guidelines. In this case, leadership comes from the ability to get the most out of what is legally allowed.

If a business were to operate with such rigid parameters, there would be zero growth, employees would not be challenged, and the quality of the product would suffer immeasurably. Inevitably, a Going out of Business sign would soon be hanging in the window. This is where a system of employee interviews, product quality worksheets, and company growth statistics are beneficial to determining the type of manager on site. There is not always an outside cause for declining performance. Many times the cause lies in those making decisions as managers, who aim to stay within the parameters, versus the leaders, who aim to stretch the boundaries of performance. A popular quote that is often paraphrased is that "the success of a company goes from the bottom up, while the attitude of a company goes from the top down." Subordinates will function only at the ability with which they are led.

## The Peter Principle

One of the ways in which managers fail at becoming effective leaders is due to the concept of the Peter Principle. This concept, named after Canadian researcher Dr. Laurence J. Peter, is an "observation that in a hierarchy people tend to rise to 'their level of incompetence.' Thus, as people are promoted, they become progressively less effective because good performance in one job does not guarantee similar performance in another."[1]

A case could be made that a major contributor to the rise of the Peter Principle is nepotism and "buddy system" promotions. It is safe to say that almost everyone in every profession has been witness to the Peter Principle at one time or another. No place of employment is exempt from it. Small family businesses rely on family and friends in order to keep costs low, but the trend goes as far as government

---

[1] Business Dictionary, *Peter Principle*, accessed January 13, 2016, www. businessdictionary.com/definition.

agencies in which political appointees are tasked with crucial jobs that are clearly beyond their capability, yet they serve a particular agenda. Whether these promotions are granted out of necessity or personal gain, the outcome is often the same: failed leadership contributing to a failing business.

It can hardly be said that nepotism and the buddy system are new concepts. Undoubtedly they have existed for as long as mankind has. The problem in the modern era is that levels of competition in each profession are so high that failing leadership can not only destroy a business but also drastically impact workers who may have limited skills outside of their current positions. The effect of the Peter Principle has further impact, as hundreds of families may face the possibility of poverty due to poor decision making from the leadership role. This can easily be noted as a dramatic lack of leadership, and even poor management. For now, the parameters of success in the company cannot even be maintained. Unfortunately, in a politically correct era, in which hurting someone's feelings has been deemed hateful, these promotions are never corrected through the use of demotion. Rather, a new position must be created for an additional employee to help correct the shortcomings already present. This added expense is an unnecessary economic load on what may already be a quickly sinking ship. Leadership has failed. The Peter Principle is not a concept that is strictly attached to the business world, however; it also applies to families. These same concepts of promotion and demotion are not given by others; rather, they are a result of the choices we make, and these choices affect everyone.

*Theological Significance*

In our human way of viewing certain characteristics and positions, we oftentimes fail to simplify the concepts to their basic foundations. The most fundamental place to begin any thought of leadership is with the family unit. How many times has the expression been said,

"I manage the household?" In an era of declining moral culture, it is imperative to do more than manage the family; we must *lead* the family.

By using terminology such as "family manager," we are essentially downgrading the roles we play for our children and our spouses. Are our only responsibilities to provide food, shelter, clothing, and allowances? The family unit is akin to a little-thought-of corporation; it is a microcosm of life within the outside world, and it is the first taste children get of how successful entities can run. Western culture has slowly and subtly demoralized the family unit into a dysfunctional example that children now take into the workplace, the military, and their own families as examples of what to do and how to succeed. The result of this can only end one way, and that is in failure.

Scripturally, the family unit is essential. The vast majority of people, whether Christian or not, can spout off some of the Ten Commandments. One of the most popularly quoted is the fifth commandment, "Honor your father and your mother, that your days may be long upon the land which the Lord your God is giving you" (Exodus 20:12).[2]

There is a precedent to the order of importance in these commandments. God declares with the very first commandment that *He* is the Lord, and there should be *no* others before Him. Throughout Judeo-Christian beliefs, this is the defining law. There is none higher than God. So, given that number five pertains to the family unit—ahead of murder, adultery, theft, lying, and coveting— this demonstrates how important the family unit is to God. Take heed throughout scripture that the traditional nuclear family is what God references. Proverbs 1:8 furthers the message of family: "Listen, my son, to your father's instruction and do not forsake your mother's teaching." These are fundamental passages for the Christian family

---

[2] All quoted scripture is taken from the New King James Version unless otherwise noted.

5

that demonstrate that the role of a parent goes far beyond mere management. You are tasked with leadership!

It is important to note that implying special significance to each of the Ten Commandments is not something that is scripturally specified in any way other than interpretation. To a Holy God, all sin is equal, and thus breaking one commandment is just as bad as breaking any other. What is intriguing is that God dictated this particular order for a reason. That reason may be as simple as ensuring that mankind understood without a doubt that number one was absolutely the most important, or that the key to a successful life of peace and harmony lay in "If you do this first, then this, you will find peace." Regardless of reason, family is the cornerstone of God's relationship with His creation.

The following pages will display several examples of leadership principles for the family unit from a theological perspective. Joshua demonstrated his leadership not only of the nation of Israel but also of his family when he declared with a strong voice, "But as for *me* and *my* house, *we* will serve the Lord" (Joshua 24:15, author emphasis added). Joshua did not take a management approach to his family and say, "These are the guidelines I'd like you to follow." Instead he took a leadership role and declared his position over his house: "*We will* serve the Lord!"

If you view your role in your own household only as that of a manager, you are seriously devaluing the role you were given, and subsequently, the example your children will follow is one of passive existence. Embrace your family as CEO. Lead in order to set the examples that will not only benefit your children in the home but will also embed in them the necessary skills and mindset to succeed in the world as adults. If children are our future, it is up to us to ensure they are equipped to take the mantle of responsibility.

How does the Peter Principle apply to families? In the business world, there are many examples of negligent promotions given to individuals who are not necessarily suited for the job. Families have the same issue, only it isn't a case of promotion but a choice of self-gratification. Through the last part of the twentieth century and the beginning of the twenty-first century, how many children are brought into this world as planned babies to married parents? We do not need statistics to see that the number is overwhelmingly small.

The enjoyable act has just produced an unplanned consequence, and two people who were not necessarily prepared for parenthood are now thrust into the job on a "learn as you go" basis. Financial hardships, living situations, marital decisions, and keeping the child are all decisions that are crucial in a very short period of time. How one reacts determines one's level of leadership in their family. For the man, does he admit his role and stick around, embracing the opportunity to take on the new challenge, or does he demote himself and flee from the responsibility he had a hand in creating? Does the woman decide to keep the child and embrace the motherhood she is not prepared for?

When the Peter Principle is present, accountability and responsibility seldom are. Those who embrace their new position, take advice from others, and desire to do good, buck the trend and become effective leaders and role models—what every child needs.

# FAITH

*Secular Significance*

The idea of faith is often never considered to be a principle of leadership in the secular world. Many people even struggle with the concept of faith in the theological world, despite faith being a cornerstone of every religion. In fact, faith is best thought of as the foundational cornerstone on which all principles of leadership can be built. Why? Because it is in faith that leaders are able to demonstrate all other principles—faith in themselves and faith in their subordinates.

Sometimes faith can be misinterpreted and misapplied. A person in charge may believe he is demonstrating faith in his subordinates and may believe he has faith in himself. However, actions speak louder than words. With reference back to the Peter Principle and methods of promotion, someone who is given a position that is not truly warranted can often take on a false sense of bravado. This manifests itself to employees as nothing more than a narcissistic attitude. Whether there is any validity to the charge of narcissism is irrelevant, as the leader is judged upon what is witnessed in his example.

What is it about faith that makes it a foundational element on which everything else can be built? Faith is all-encompassing. Trust, integrity, humility, communication, and vision, to name a few, are all things that a leader can display through example by having faith.

In many areas, unfortunately, leaders can be found to have George Costanza syndrome. This reference from episode sixteen of the sixth season ("The Beard") of the popular television series *Seinfeld* sees Jerry forced to pass a lie detector test, and he seeks assistance from his friend George, who says, "Jerry, just remember: it's not a lie if *you* believe it."

Misinterpreted faith is found in leaders who fail to see or admit that they are not living up to the same standard they are trying to set for others. *They* believe it; therefore, it must be true. In the business world, this belief can spell doom for a company. For more hostile workplaces, such as law enforcement and combat operations, this attitude can be fatal. The following pages will delve more deeply into the elements contained in the idea of faith. I hope the connection will resonate with everyone.

*Theological Significance*

Faith plays a much deeper role in the theological aspect of leadership than it does in the secular realm for no reason other than its cornerstone position. However, the significance of faith cannot be underestimated in its role in the secular world. Faith is most often recognized in the world of religion. All world religions call upon adherents to possess faith in the higher power that controls their destiny. Faith is the fundamental building block for spiritual growth as a person and is the prime element for building successful families. Faith is complete confidence, trust, or belief not based on proof. In the secular world, proof is required to validate everything. Our minds have been twisted through our culture to accept only things that can be scientifically explained, and regardless of the sensibility of the explained "truth," man accepts the expert opinion of a scholar.

We are told that science proves the creation of man via evolution. Our leaders endorse this opinion; therefore, schools teach this opinion. Creationism, being based on faith, finds no home in our public schools. Is this due to the misinterpreted statement of Thomas

Jefferson declaring a separation between church and state, or is it a deeper problem of mankind not being able to accept that some things neither have nor require proof? Since the time of the Age of Enlightenment, man has set into motion an agenda for eliminating God from His rightful place. The humanist mind is unable to accept that there is a higher power than man.

Those with faith in a creator often struggle to find harmony in a secular world where the Judeo-Christian God in particular is vilified. Where lies the rationale in accepting the claims of Islam, Buddhism, or Hinduism as legitimate beliefs that must be treated with respect while disavowing anything related to the God of Judeo-Christian faith? Since 1715, when the Age of Enlightenment is deemed to have gotten its start, man has been on a mission to live without faith and rather has placed his trust in the proof of science. That is a mere three hundred years of man's existence!

Prior to this period, faith played a crucial role in man's life, where gods were prayed to for every aspect of society and culture. The Creationist viewpoint of man's existence having lasted roughly six thousand years means that faith was fundamental for approximately fifty-seven hundred years. Even more astounding is the time frame attributed by science. "While our ancestors have been around for about six million years, the modern form of humans only evolved about 200,000 years ago. Civilization as we know it is only about 6,000 years old, and industrialization started in the earnest only in the 1800s."[3]

What science purports to be our ancestors is not relevant in relation to our thoughts on modern man. The modern form of man is deemed by science to have been in existence for 200,000 years, so theoretically, man relied on faith over science for 199,700 years. The obvious connection between Creationism and evolution appears to

---

[3] Elizabeth Howell, "How Long Have Humans Been On Earth," *Universe Today*, January 19, 2015, http://www.universetoday.com/38125/how-long-have-humans-been-on-earth/.

exist in the number 6,000. If science accepts civilization as having developed 6,000 years ago, the concept of man's creation at 6,000 years ago is not unfathomable when one considers God's role in developing human society.

It is this belief in God that allows us to focus on the theological significance of leadership in these sections. What you will discover is that all principles of leadership are displayed throughout scripture. If you have faith in a higher power, you can be assured that the example set forth in scripture is true and accurate. For every principle of leadership you encounter throughout this book, you will see an example of a biblical figure possessing such a trait. Abraham is the first example regarding faith. What is it about Abraham that makes him special in regard to leadership?

The genealogy that the book of Genesis gives us from Adam through Abraham offers interesting insight. Genesis 6 tells us that by the time of Noah, corruption had taken over the earth. Idolatry and pagan worship were becoming too common, and God was grieved over His creation of man. Noah was the tenth generation from creation, so it took ten generations for mankind to forget the greatness of God and begin to rely on paganism. The deep regret that God had for creating man led to a worldwide judgment, culminating in the flood. Only one man was deemed righteous and allowed to survive along with his family, and that man was Noah.

Once the floodwaters subsided, the genealogy of mankind continued from Noah through Abraham and is listed in Genesis 10 and 11. Undoubtedly, the first several generations after Noah were well aware of God's judgment against man and lived righteous lives in the eyes of God. Abraham, ironically enough, was the tenth generation from Noah and the twentieth generation from creation. We see that it took mankind ten generations to become so corrupt that God felt the need to destroy the human race He had taken such pride and joy in creating. We see that in only another ten generations, the world was corrupt again, and paganism was beginning to be practiced with regularity.

Instead of destroying mankind again, God opted for another approach to maintain the relationship with man that was in His original plan. In a land of pagan worship, God found righteousness in a man named Abram and called to him. Genesis 12 recounts the story of Abram's calling and what Abram had to do solely on faith. The Bible is unclear as to exactly how much was known of God the Creator to Abram at this time in history. God's direction to Abram was to leave his father's house with his wife and servants and travel to a land that God would show him. In today's world, how many people would have the faith necessary to pick up everything they owned and travel to a new land they knew nothing about and rely solely on faith that a voice they were hearing would fulfill the promise of not only blessing them but also blessing all the families of the earth through them?

Just as Noah surely encountered ridicule and criticism ten generations earlier as he built an ark in faith, which no one else could possibly understand, Abram likely encountered the same type of ridicule and criticism. His family and friends must have thought he was crazy for venturing out through the wilderness with all of his possessions without knowing where or why he was going. Here are two examples of extreme faith exhibited by both Noah and Abram: Through Abram's obedience to God, his name was changed to Abraham, and he became a leader of not only his family but also the people of his tribe and the generations of people that followed directly after him. Is there a better testament to the importance of faith in a position of leadership than what was demonstrated by Abraham? Whether it does so secularly or theologically, faith becomes our driving foundational principle of leadership.

## Vision

*Secular Significance*

The concept of vision is a good principle to apply under faith. Those with vision are often called dreamers. With that descriptor, couldn't it be concluded that all people share the vision of leadership because all people have hopes and dreams they wish to achieve? Yes! The difference between the leader with vision and everyone else lies in the persistence to see that vision through to completion.

Vision must also be shared. A leader who does not share information, or his vision, with his subordinates is at a disadvantage. In order to be successful, everyone must be on the same page. In an office environment, the person in charge has others who must be in sync with the leadership vision. A major hurdle that must be overcome by every manager with a vision is ego. Does the person in a leadership role have the capability to delegate? Or does the leader possess the attitude that he is smarter than everyone else? If the leaders believe that they are smarter than everyone else, then they will put themselves on a pedestal and begin dictating the orders of a vision instead of explaining in detail what the long-term goals of the vision are.

What are goals? Are there clear-cut goals within each vision? One of the worst mistakes any manager can make is believing that he is in a leadership position and that he can lead effectively when he refuses to share the goals in the details set forth in the vision of the company's new direction. Employees must feel invested in the work that they do, and in order for that to happen, employees must be aware of the details of the vision. No employee of any value will do his best work if he feels as if he is being treated like a child. The concept of "do what I said because I said so" is a recipe for disaster.

Let's create an example. A general manager overseeing a midsized manufacturing facility assigns the plant manager role to someone who will go along with whatever is asked of him, never questioning if it is for the best interest of the facility. Does this general manager feel the need to share all the minute details of his vision for the entire company? In the event that the general manager does share the details of the company's vision with the facility's manager, does the facility manager then take the responsibility to share those details with the department heads? Does each department head then share the details with the bottom-line employees tasked with fulfilling the mission? If the details of the vision are shared all the way to the bottom, the odds of success for this facility greatly increase.

What happens to the success of a facility if any one of these leaders decides that the need to share details with anyone else below him is not important? What if the sharing of details stops at the facility manager? Now not only are the bottom-line employees left out of the understanding of the vision, but the department heads are as well. How does an employee effectively do his job when his immediate supervisor is unable to answer any questions pertaining to the task at hand? Now let's compound the question of leadership and vision with an additional twist. What happens to the facility if the facility manager decides that he can wear multiple hats as well as being the facility manager?

A department head has been eliminated, which theoretically should remove an impediment from the flow of information between the manager and the employees. However, the situation of sharing the details of the vision has not changed. All that has happened is that there is now a direct route from the employee in the department to the facility manager, who is now overextended in his leadership role. In leadership circles, it has been recognized that a leader is most effective when overseeing between five and seven people. This is the reason that delegation and sharing the details of the company's vision is critical for success. In our example, not only has the vision not been shared, but dissension and controversy now arise over the removal of a department head. The employee no longer has a buffer zone for dissent, and the employee is left with no understanding of why the decision was made to remove his department head when no details of the vision have been passed down.

Does this sound as if the employees will be invested in this facility? Where is the leadership flaw? Does the flaw lie with the facility manager, who decided to cease the flow of information and remove a department head, or does the flaw lie with the general manager, who chose plant managers incapable of making proper leadership decisions? To repeat the well-known quote, "The attitude of a company goes from the top down, and the success of a company goes from the bottom up."

Ultimately the primary leadership flaw lies with the general manager for not ensuring the people directly under him were capable of carrying out the assigned tasks set forth in the vision. On a smaller scale, the leadership flaw for the facility lies with the facility manager for a couple of reasons. One—this manager has taken on too much responsibility. Two—this manager has failed to treat his subordinates as productive members of the team, opting to give them information on a need-to-know basis while keeping them out of the loop of the overall vision of the company. The success of this facility will now be determined by the attitude that has filtered down through the layers of management. The moral of the story is to be open, trusting, and confident that all of the people under you will put the plan in place once they understand the vision being set forth.

Vision represents the dreams and concepts of those in charge, and to ensure that the vision is realized, all goals must be presented throughout the organization and specified in detail so that every member of the team can embrace the ultimate goal. The foresight of a good leader will enable all potential issues to be addressed in a timely and efficient manner.

## *Theological Significance*

Do you have a vision for your family? What are your family expectations? As the leader of the family, it is up to you to have the vision of which direction your family will move. All parents have hopes and dreams of what they would like to see their children accomplish in life. Do you foster an environment for that child to embrace what your vision actually is? Do you push your vision onto your children? There is a fine line between living out a vision and living your life through your child. Much like a business, your spouse and children must understand the fine elements of your vision.

Many stories are told of children who go in directions radically different from what their parents envision, because they feel that the parents' dreams are being forced onto them. One example of the proper way to guide a child is the nuclear family that engages in activities together. The parent, as the leader of the family, will go out of his or her way to gently guide the child in a direction that not only strengthens the child but also the family. Each parent may have his or her own vision of how he or she would like to see each child grow, but both must operate as a team in order to ensure there is no confusion of expectations placed on the child.

In a family that stresses moral values, going to church on Sunday may be a fundamental family activity. Perhaps the parents have a vision of their son becoming a pastor someday. The parents use the gentle guidance of a Sunday morning church service to instill a potential desire in their child. The worst thing the parents could do as their children aged would be to continue to force their will upon their children. Children, much like peers in an office, need to have a complete understanding of the vision set forth for them. In this way, perhaps the son, of his own volition, will have the desire to follow the example set forth by his parents and become the minister that they desired him to become.

First Timothy 3:4–7 briefly discusses the idea of vision within a family unit, taking into account ego and one of the seven deadly sins—pride. Let's take a quick look at what these verses tell us. "One who rules his own house well, having his children in submission with all reverence (for if a man does not know how to rule his own house, how will he take care of the church of God?); not a novice, lest being puffed up with pride he fall into the same condemnation as the devil."

On the surface, this seems to run contradictory to our previous statement that parents should not force their will upon their children. However, "submission" in this case does not refer to forcing life-changing decisions upon your children; rather, it refers to respect and obedience. As God offers man free will to choose between right and wrong, He also requires submission of all of His children if they are to grow up successful in faith.

God's vision for mankind is for everyone to be able to share in the glory of eternity and God's presence. He does not force his vision upon man but does require submission to His will in order to achieve this vision. In much the same way, the leader of the home is tasked with requiring submission of the children if they are to grow up successful and be able to obtain the vision set forth by the parents. Also, in much the same way, parents allow children to have free will as they get older. The path that they choose will be their own, but the success of that path will be determined by whether or not the vision was followed to completion.

A good example of vision can be found in the Old Testament prophets. Their visions were literal visions—not of something new to be achieved through innovative methods, but of God's plans. All of the Old Testament prophets were commissioned by God to help lead the Israelites in righteousness. These prophets performed an essential role in this time period by being the intermediaries between God and His people. Prior to Pentecost—when the Holy Spirit came to fill believers and fulfill the roles of intercessor, advocate, and teacher—the prophets were the method of delivering God's Word to the people.

Most of the time, the message being delivered was one of warning. The Israelite prophets understood God's plan and assumed the mission of delivering to the people the news that the people's repentance was required. Much like a good leader in a business environment is responsible for delivering the details of his vision to his subordinates in order to achieve success, the prophets laid out in detail what the people of God must do in order to find their salvation. Also, much like the business world, when subordinates fail to take directives, calamity occurs. A company could soon be out of business in such a case, and in a similar fashion, the ancient Israelites found themselves essentially out of business.

It is important to know what the mission of the ancient Israelites actually was. They were given a simple task to be the chosen people of God through whom Jesus would be born, and to be the light of nations by serving as missionaries for God. This long-term vision was hinted to Abraham when he was told that through him all the nations of the world would be blessed. The prophet Isaiah declared the following as the voice of the Lord in Isaiah 56 6–7: "Also the sons of the foreigner who join themselves to the Lord, to serve him, and to love the name of the Lord, to be his servants-everyone who keeps from defiling the Sabbath, and holds fast My covenant-Even them I will bring to My holy mountain, and make them joyful in My house of prayer, their burnt offerings and their sacrifices will be accepted on My altar; for My house shall be called a house of prayer for **all nations**."

Clearly Isaiah is revealing a vision given to him by God to let the people know the details of the plan which they were tasked with carrying out. All nations were to come to Jerusalem to worship the Lord. This is a clear-cut mission statement that the purpose the Israelites were to serve was to be emissaries and missionaries for God to all the world, Jew and Gentile alike.

We can now see the importance of vision in leadership, not only from a business perspective but also in the family unit and historically in scripture. We can also see how the element of vision falls within the greater concept of faith. Every leader in any situation who possesses a vision for something better sees the fulfillment of the vision only through faith—faith that the vision is correct, faith in subordinates to carry out the details of the vision, and faith that as a leader he has put his people in the proper positions to succeed.

# INTEGRITY

*Secular Significance*

Integrity is another foundational principle that all leaders must possess. In order for any leader to be successful and to be thought of as a leader, all aspects of a person's life must coincide with the message he preaches. Is it unfair to say all aspects of a person's life must coincide? It probably is, to some degree. There are special circumstances and situations in which a person's knowledge base and skill set are the only things that matter in accomplishing a mission. For instance, to a soldier the most important aspect of a combat leader is the capability of fulfilling the mission and getting the troops home safely. A foot soldier is not concerned about his combat leader's personal life as much as he is about surviving the mission he is tasked to fulfill.

These are unique circumstances that do not show up regularly in the civilian world. Even a successful combat leader, when entering the civilian world, cannot solely rely on his military successes if fatal flaws can be seen in other aspects of his life. Like all principles of leadership, integrity is a key part of the mix, as it is intertwined with every other principle. Who is the more successful leader—the person who says "Do as I say, not as I do" or the person who lives to the same standard he preaches?

Not all leadership positions are created equally. Integrity, however, carries serious consequences in every leadership position.

One type of leader, for example, is a government representative. This person chooses to take on a leadership position by running for office and is elected by peers to make crucial decisions that affect everyone. How important is integrity to this individual? It appears from what we see in the news that integrity is not a concept that is often taken into consideration when we go to the polls. Our duty is to elect someone who reflects our value system and will do the job that serves our interests as constituents. When and if we actually take the time to examine the background and actions of a person running for office, we can sometimes be stunned by our own ignorance in the voting booth. It seems as if we routinely elect people to positions of leadership and tasking them with making laws that affect our everyday lives, though these same individuals are incapable of successfully managing their own lives and households.

Is integrity an important concept in this position? How about the position of church pastor? Is integrity important in the person that you depend on to provide you with spiritual strength? How effective of a leader could a pastor be if his name suddenly appeared on a sex offender list? Would you question the spiritual guidance from someone who had been through multiple divorces? Some of these things do not necessarily make the individual a bad person, but they do leave an impression with those following that this leader embraces the "do as I say, not as I do" mentality. In the business world, "do as I say, not as I do" can have just as damaging side effects.

Any person in a position of leadership is automatically granted the respect of the position. It is assumed by anyone in a subordinate position that the person in leadership possesses a skill set, mentality, and value system that distinguishes him above everyone else to be qualified to be a leader. Oftentimes this is a mistake of confusing management with leadership. As mentioned earlier, just because someone is a good manager does not mean that he possesses the qualities necessary to be a good leader.

Let's look at an example. A supervisor approaches an employee and commends him not only on the job he does but on other achievements accomplished outside of work that make the employee more valuable. The supervisor then makes a promise to the employee he they will do whatever is possible to ensure the employee is promoted within the company to a position that has been earned through diligent work. Initially the effect on the employee is tremendous, as the ego gets stroked a little and the employee senses that all his hard work has not gone unnoticed. Weeks and months go past, and the employee does not receive the new position promised. What is the reaction of the employee? The first assumption is that the supervisor has lied when other people less qualified are given bumps within the company. How does the future work ethic of the employee change? Should the future work ethic of the employee change? To the employee, it seems as though all of his hard work has been in vain. The supervisor is now considered untrustworthy by the employee, and any future compliment is deemed to be a lie as well.

A supervisor with this reputation is detrimental to employee morale and incredibly damaging to the business in an age where word of mouth and social media define perceptions. Just as damaging is when the chain of command is broken and a higher-up confronts an employee with damning remarks about that employee's immediate supervisor. How can the employee respond? Either the allegations of the higher-up are taken as truth and the immediate supervisor loses all credibility within his department, or the employee is left feeling vulnerable in knowing that if his supervisor could be thrown under the bus so easily, it is only a matter of time until the employee is also thrown under the bus.

These are just a few brief examples of the importance of integrity in someone in a leadership position. Integrity consists of many elements that will be discussed later, strengthening the point that all principles of leadership are intertwined in creating a successful leader. Integrity in the workplace means that the person in authority is trustworthy, reliable, and willing to live within the same guidelines that are demanded of the subordinates. Sometimes integrity and character are thought to be the same, but there are subtle differences. One of my favorite sayings about the difference between the two is that integrity is character in the heart. While character is a way of recognizing a person's attributes, integrity digs deeper, as it seeks to discover consistency between what a person says and what a person does. Integrity has the potential to be the defining trait in a leader that will determine the degree to which he is followed.

## Ethics

A principle that goes along with integrity is ethics. A person who displays solid integrity will also display sound ethics. In the business world, ethics contains issues such as discrimination, insider trading, and bribery. Issues such as these could also be referred to as issues of honor and responsibility. A responsible leader would never jeopardize what is best for his business by engaging in illicit practices. "Honesty" is synonymous with the aforementioned word "trustworthy." An honest leader practices what he preaches and puts the reputation of the business ahead of everything else. In this regard, simple ethics are an offshoot of integrity.

## Core Values

All successful organizations must possess a set of core values. These values represent what your business stands for. They are reflected in your leadership and must filter down to all of your employees. Each branch of the military possesses a set of core values that must be embraced by everyone in each branch. Religious institutions also possess core values, and these values are represented in scripture. What is it about core values that are essential for success? For one, core values are unifying. They set a level of expectation to be followed by everyone in order to function as a team. If a member of the team does not embrace the core values of the organization, that one person becomes a distraction whose attitude will fester and spread throughout the unit.

A few examples of core values are integrity, excellence, respect, honor, courage, commitment, loyalty, selfless service, and duty. These are core values represented by the US military; however, by no means are they limited exclusively to the military. Every organization, whether business or social—or even smaller, such as the family unit—should embrace these simple core values. It is evident that a group of people possessing these characteristics will achieve far more than those that don't. These core values are a good baseline to build upon, but one does not have to be limited to these values alone. Perhaps there are other keywords that build on those listed above that a business may adopt in order to achieve its particular vision.

How important do these core values appear to be in relation to leadership? As stated, the whole purpose of leadership is to achieve success by guiding others in the most effective and efficient manner. Would it be easy to follow a superior who did not display integrity, respect, or loyalty? In order to most effectively foster a team-like environment, the core values chosen to represent your particular business should be written out and posted around the facility for all to see. These values should be stressed not only in word but also in action. Thus far, having touched on only a few principles, is it becoming evident how effective leadership must contain each principle and how the chain reaction would follow with the loss of one? A true leader must stand for something, and that something should be reflected in values, ethics, integrity, vision, and faith.

*Theological Significance*

My mother used to frequently quote a saying of my grandfather, and I believe this to be a very insightful and timeless saying: "As the family goes so goes the nation." My grandfather was a marine in World War II who fought valiantly, island-hopping across the

Pacific. It was not only the accomplishments of this generation that gave them the title "the greatest generation"; it was also their insight gained from life experiences and family values. In the twenty-first century, I can take my grandfather's quote a step further by adding "so goes the world." The rise and fall of cultures can be witnessed in the rise and fall of families. This is by no means intended to discredit so many of the outstanding people who have come from single-parent homes; it is merely a reflection of how our society has drastically changed in the past thirty years.

In reference to my grandfather's quote, we can look at one constant throughout all of history: the family is the foundational stone on which societies and cultures are built. Each generation is a reflection on the one that came before it and the values that preceding generation instilled. Earlier we took note of Noah and Abraham, two righteous individuals who had faith, vision, integrity, and leadership over their families. Much as in the times of Noah and Abraham, the further away mankind moves generationally from righteousness, the more corrupt our society becomes. Mankind in general has always suffered the predisposition of the original sin, and in time man has always sought to place himself on the top rung of order.

Every generation therefore naturally maintains smaller and smaller amounts of the lessons learned from previous generations while seeking to put their own stamp on their era. Where has this taken us? From the creation of man until the age of Enlightenment, mankind always assumed some brand of religion and deity-led influence over every aspect of life. Somehow, from the age of Enlightenment until the modern day, a short few hundred years, many in society have grown to view religion as taboo. It is this influence that has become detrimental to our families, our societies, and our culture. One important feature that has led to this mentality is the lack of leadership in the family unit. More specifically there has been a lack of integrity, ethics, and core values demonstrated for our children.

In the book of Psalms, the author recounts in chapter 78, verse 72, "So he shepherded them according to the integrity of his heart, and guided them by the skillfulness of his hands." It is easy to pick out the keyword to focus on in this verse, and that word is "integrity." Throughout this chapter of Psalms, the author recounts how God's chosen people became disobedient, were taken into slavery, were delivered from their oppression, and were given a leader to follow. That leader's name was David.

Those who are somewhat familiar with the story of David may be saying, "Wait a minute, how can you use David as an example of integrity when he committed adultery, lied, and had Bathsheba's husband killed on the battlefield?" On the surface this is a pretty damning argument against what we know about integrity. However, let's look more at David. When David was a young shepherd boy, the prophet Samuel was told by God to anoint young David to be the future king of Israel. David was faithful and obedient to God, and faithful and obedient to King Saul, fulfilling his role as a selfless servant to the king. When Saul became disobedient to God, he was killed in battle, and he passed the crown of Israel to David. In David's faithfulness and obedience, God delivered all the enemies of Israel into David's hands, allowing David to strengthen all the tribes of Israel as one nation.

As is the nature of man, David fell victim to pride. It became David's belief that as king he could have whatever he wanted, and what David wanted was Bathsheba, the wife of one of his loyal soldiers. While Bathsheba's husband Uriah was away in battle, David took Bathsheba in lust. When it became known that Bathsheba was with David's child, David recalled Uriah and attempted to coerce Uriah into being intimate with his wife, thus hiding the fact that David was the actual father of the child. When Uriah refused the comforts of his wife, David sent him back into battle carrying a note for the general to put Uriah at the front of the hottest battle so that he would be killed. Upon the death of Uriah, David took Bathsheba as his wife.

This hardly sounds like a leader worthy of the principle of integrity, but David was a man, and as a man, he fell victim to man's sin. If this were the end of the story, the example set forth by David would promote zero integrity, a severe lack of leadership, and an extremely poor example for the children of Israel to follow. Luckily, this is not the end of the story. The prophet Nathan approached David and chastised him, relaying the curse that God was putting on David's household. The child conceived in adultery would die as punishment for David's sin. David reacted in a way that that re-instilled his integrity. He dropped to the floor, laid prostrate, and repented for the sin he had committed with Bathsheba. He begged God for a new heart, for forgiveness, and to not let him fall out of God's favor. This took integrity. The king of Israel humbled himself before a higher power and vowed his faithfulness and obedience to God. As his reward, it was his son Solomon, born to Bathsheba, who would follow David on the throne, building God's temple and become the wisest king on earth.

What can we learn from David? We learn that we are only human, we make mistakes, and life goes on. It is the manner in which we proceed with life that provides rewards or consequences. As parents and leaders of the home, it is our responsibility to acknowledge our mistakes and use them as teachable moments for the future in raising our children. All parents wish to see their children achieve greater things than themselves. No parent wishes to hold his or her child back from succeeding in life. In order for children to have success in their adult lives, they need embrace the lessons of their parents. These lessons begin with integrity.

As we step outside the circle of immediate family, another important quote becomes essential to this lesson: "It takes a village to raise a child." Most people have heard this quote before and are familiar with its meaning, but let's add to the perspective. When we acknowledge that the family unit is the foundational stone on which society is built, we also acknowledge that the influences from outside our family unit can be very powerful. While the most important lessons of example come from parents and grandparents, another major influence on children is the community in which they grow up. Integrity is not just an important principle for parents to represent; it is also important for the community. Are you a strong leader in your family? Do you have strong neighbors that represent the same values you are teaching your children? If not, the role of parenting becomes even more critical than it already was.

### Ethics

When it comes to family ethics, they really are no difference from business ethics when we consider honor and responsibility. The apostle Paul discussed what makes an ethically righteous man in his letter to Titus: "If a man is blameless, the husband of one wife, having faithful children not accused of dissipation or insubordination. For a bishop must be blameless, as a steward of God, not self-willed, not quick-tempered, not given to wine, not violent, not greedy for money, but hospitable, a lover of what is good, sober minded, just, holy, self-controlled, holding fast the faithful word as he has been taught, that he may be able, by sound doctrine, both to exhort and convict those who contradict" (Titus 1:6–9).

Although Paul uses the phrase "a bishop must be blameless," these qualities are actually essential for everyone. There is always misinterpretation when it comes to aspects of scripture, such as when Paul says, "not given to wine." A literal translation of the short four words is an example of what some people use to claim that the Bible is contradictory. On the one hand, throughout the Bible righteous people are seen drinking wine regularly, but here Paul is saying man should not be given to wine. This would be an example of proof-texting—something that is very popular for people searching for answers and not understanding the actual meaning of what they are reading. "Not given to wine," merely refers to drunkenness. It is not good to be an alcoholic, for those who are given to wine meet the conditions of being alcoholics, and they often struggle with many of the other characteristics Paul talks about. Take a quick look back at the list of things Paul says an ethical man should be, and see how many of these characteristics would be very difficult if not completely unattainable for someone suffering from alcoholism. Proof-texting is very dangerous when it comes to reading scripture, because scripture can never mean what it never meant. I believe that this example of ethical behavior, if it were to be employed by every head of household, would lead to a very different mindset in the next generation.

## Core Values

Core values are universal. Core values are individual principles. While core values can be found at the heart of every successful organization, they begin within the individual. Whether the person displaying core values is a high-ranking executive or a bottom-level underling, the way a person lives his life sets the tone for how others around that individual will respond. Since core values are reflected in an individual and are universal, the same ones are used and effective in any environment—including, most specifically, a family unit.

When we think of ourselves as employees and notice how we respond to those around us who may or may not display core values, and we realize how important these values become to our morale and our work ethic, we can begin to see their importance within the family unit. The future of our children is dependent upon the values set forth in the home, and those values are best enforced through example. The "do as I say, not as I do" principle carries much more weight in the family environment than it does in the work environment. Regardless of what children are told, whether consciously or subconsciously, they will always absorb the example they witness. By embracing the concept of core values and focusing on them every day, the individual will become not only a better person but also a better leader for others to follow.

In essence, we must all stand for something. There are two scriptural versus I enjoy that are representative of core values and standing for something. The first is 2 Timothy 2:15–17, which says, "Be diligent to present yourself approved to God, a worker who does not need to be ashamed, rightly dividing the word of truth. But shun profane and idle babblings, or they will increase to more ungodliness. And their message will spread like cancer ..." What is it that Paul is telling Timothy he should stand for? Timothy is being told to stand for the highest of all things—the approval of God. Many of us go through life often concerned for our reputations. Our reputations are important in our workplaces, our communities, and our families. These types of reputations that we concern ourselves with are only in the eyes of man; how much more concerned should we be that our reputations are approved by God?

Another of my favorite verses in reference to standing for something is paraphrased repeatedly when a service member passes, and that verse is John 10:11: "I am the good shepherd. The good Shepherd gives his life for the sheep." Jesus uttered these words to the Pharisees who were questioning him, and today we often hear people say that there is no greater love than when someone lays down his life for another. In life people tend to pick and choose which text they feel can make themselves and others feel good while ignoring all the rest, but in reality this is not just a verse about feeling good and saying the right thing; rather, it is a core value for standing for something greater than yourself.

There are numerous examples in the Bible of righteous men and women who stand for something. These are people of integrity, with unwavering faith, who are willing to sacrifice anything and everything in this world for the greater good. One final example that I will mention here is the prophet Daniel. Daniel's enemies attempted to trap him because he was a favorite of King Darius and was placed above all the governors in the kingdom of the Medes and Persians. These enemies came together and established a statute to decree that whoever prays to any god or man for thirty days other than Darius would be cast into the lion's den. Daniel, as a faithful servant of God, continued to pray, as his enemies knew he would, violating the royal decree. Darius was heavily grieved knowing that his decree was to be used against his trusted advisor, Daniel. After Daniel was cast into the den, the king spent the night fasting in his palace. The concept of fasting was not unique to the Israelites, but it is not unreasonable to believe that Daniel's faith and religious practices did not have an influence on Darius. In Daniel 6:16, Darius says to Daniel, "Your God, whom you serve continually, He will deliver you."

That simple statement shows us that even Darius was a believer in Daniel's God because of the wonders Daniel had performed. Daniel was at peace in the lion's den, and the next morning when Darius awoke and rushed to the den, he found Daniel alive and well. In verse 22 Daniel says, "My God sent his angel and shut the lion's mouths that they have not hurt me, because I was found innocent before him; and also, O king, I have done no wrong before you."

Daniel stood for something righteous and was delivered. As children of God, He loves you just as much, so you must ask yourself, "Would He not save me from my trials and afflictions if I stood for something good and righteous also?"

# ACCOUNTABILITY

"Accountability" is a term many people think they embrace, and deep inside they may believe that they hold this value. There are many levels we can apply to accountability that make accountability an extremely important principle of leadership. Given that the principles of leadership are so easily intertwined, working together to foster the highest results, it is practically impossible to say that one thing is more important than another. Individuals vary, however, and for some people the ability to put one principle ahead of another is very simple. Personally, I put faith slightly ahead of everything else because I believe everything else falls slightly underneath it. In my eyes, all of the other principles are equal.

I recently finished a wonderfully written book, which I would highly recommend to other readers, about leadership. As was mentioned earlier, the Internet and the bookstores are full of people's ideas about leadership, and I think embracing only one source is never enough. Various circumstances offer various opportunities for teachable moments, and in these moments, new ideas that fall within common principles can be added to one's repertoire. The book I recently finished is written by two Navy SEALs, Mr. Jocko Willink and Mr. Leif Babin, and is called *Extreme Ownership: How U.S. Navy Seals Lead and Win*. The reason I choose to mention this book is because of the title. "Extreme ownership" is the ultimate phrasing for accountability. Throughout the next several sections, when I refer to accountability, try to keep the phrase "extreme ownership" in the back of your mind for the perspective that it adds.

## *Secular Significance*

In the business world, there is one trait that must always be fought against as one moves up the ladder of success and responsibility, and that trait is ego. Oftentimes in the sports world, when a team is playing well and suddenly has a very bad outing, broadcasters and journalists will refer to them as having "read their own press clippings." What this means is that the team's ego got so big they thought they could do no wrong and were subsequently knocked down. This is a similar concept in life. The more success we obtain, and the more responsibility we get without failing, the more likely we are to believe we can never fail. These are the times when bad things happen.

A very important characteristic of accountability is leading by example. If a person in control is leading by example and has an inflated ego, it is only a matter of time until he is quickly slapped back to reality. Subordinates do not respond to false bravado and a sense of self-righteousness in their leaders. A proper example to set is the exact opposite of the "do as I say, not as I do" mentality mentioned earlier. This can often be a challenge for some people who find themselves in a supervisory position. In their minds, they were given their position as a result of work they had already done and no longer feel the need to continue to do the same work. This is a tragic mistake for morale.

Those who read the book *Band of Brothers* by Stephen Ambrose or watched the miniseries of the same name will recall one key figure throughout. That man was Maj. Richard Winters. Major Winters had the respect and loyalty of his men not only because of the way he treated them or because he was tactically sound but because he believed in always leading from the front. In all of the books written by former members of Easy Company, Major Winters is always held in the highest regard. Some of the writers told the story of how Major Winters led the charge into the trenches to take out a German gun emplacement on D-Day. These guns were hidden and unknown through surveillance photos that the troops had prior to jumping into Normandy. The ability of Winters and his men to silence these guns and destroy the emplacement was critical for the thousands of men landing on the beach. Countless acts of heroism can be recounted about D-Day, and every act that was undertaken to save the life of a fellow soldier was an act of heroism. Every soldier in that trench did his job and performed an act of heroism, but it was the respect gained by Winters for leading the charge into the trench when he could have ordered someone else to go in his place that endeared him to his men throughout the war.[4]

Major Winters did not stop there but led a charge against a German company by running across an open field and onto a dike alone and in front of his men. Winters earned the respect of not only his own men but even those serving in other companies and battalions by employing a very important leadership characteristic— example. The best leaders will always be the ones in front. A very common expression used in leadership is "Never ask someone else to do something you would not do yourself." I believe almost everyone at some point in his life has performed a task under someone else that was not only unpleasant but was also performed at the direction of someone who had never done the task himself. The end result is often a very unhappy subordinate. Maj. Richard Winters was respected and followed because he set the example and he led from in front.[5]

On the flipside, a story of extremely poor leadership on the battlefield also comes from *Band of Brothers*, and once again it has to do with example. This story involves Lt. Norman Dike and his appointment by division headquarters to take over Easy Company

---

[4] Stephen E. Ambrose, *Band of Brothers: E. Company, 506th Regiment, 101st Airborne From Normandy To Hitler's Eagle's Nest* (New York: Simon & Schuster, 1992), 78–85.

[5] Ibid., 144–153.

following the promotion of Major Winters to battalion headquarters. Just prior to one of the defining moments of World War II in Europe, the Battle of the Bulge at Bastogne, Lieutenant Dike was put in charge because he was a favorite of someone higher up the chain of command who they knew that Dike required combat experience in order to gain promotion. This was the first sign of failed leadership, when division headquarters placed someone with zero experience in charge of men who had been together for almost two years and in front-line combat together for over six months.[6]

The men already had no respect for their new leader because he had never done what they had done. Throughout their time in Bastogne, under intense shelling and advances by the German army, the men seldom saw their new leader and often wondered among themselves where he was. As the level of respect and trust continued to fall, it quickly became obvious to them that their new commander was not dependable; this earned him the nickname "Foxhole" Norman.[7] Dike was not only failing to lead from the front; he was not leading at all.[8]

The issue raised its ugly head during the attack on Foy when Easy Company was tasked with routing the Germans from the village. Lieutenant Dike planned an ineffective and inefficient strategy, then compounded matters by freezing halfway through the charge leaving his men exposed. Winters, watching the scene unfold, desperately wanted to be out there leading his men from the front but was unable to because of his current position as a battalion commander. Fortunately another leader emerged to lead the charge from the front and relieve Lieutenant Dike of his duty.[9]

These two instances of men serving in the same position both offer examples of the term "example." A successful leader in any business will be the one who can most relate to the people under

---

[6] Ibid., 204.
[7] Ibid., 212.
[8] Ibid., 201–202.
[9] Ibid., 205–211.

him. The leader will be the one who volunteers to step in and plug a hole in a department every once in a while when a business is shorthanded. The leader will be the one who does just a little bit extra, even when it isn't required, to demonstrate to others what is needed. Also, the leader will be the one in front saying, "Follow me," as opposed to the one who sits in the back and says, "Do it this way."

## Humility

A true leader will always run contrary to the person displaying ego, by being the person displaying humility. Humility tends to be one of those characteristics that runs opposite of human nature, as somewhere hidden inside all of us is a little part that wants a pat on the back. Who does not want to be recognized for his hard work? Recognition is very important for morale, but in running a successful organization, the most recognition should always go to the people on the bottom. It is the humble leader who takes no credit for the success of the team but takes all of the blame for the failure of the team.

This also is something that goes against human nature but is the essence of accountability. Why was there failure? Somewhere along the line, someone did not do his job adequately, and that failure must be placed somewhere. By placing the blame on the individual who may have been the weak point, the morale of that person is significantly weakened, making it even more likely that the performance will suffer in the future. The leader who steps up and accepts the blame for either not explaining the task well enough or not giving the subordinate the proper tools to do the job successfully is respected.

I have had the pleasure of being around some wonderful leaders who never accepted any credit for the success of the team and always accepted the blame when the team failed to perform up to expectation. I have also been around some very poor leaders, and those leaders had no qualms about pointing the finger and offering more sticks than carrots. The humble leader is the one who pulls someone aside and privately asks, "What can I do to help your performance?" The humble leader is also the one who accepts all accountability without making excuses. The humble leader will always be the easiest person to identify, because the humble leader will be the one who garners the most respect from those around him, as well as the one seen working quietly and diligently in the background.

Leadership by example, through humility, requires one to not flaunt his position of authority by acting outside of the rules he imposes on others. If you want a supervisory role and you insist your employees be on time, you also must be on time. Those in subordinate roles expect to see the same standards they must adhere to in those leading them, because when those standards are broken, the person in the leadership role is often considered arrogant, as if he feels his level of importance supersedes that of the team. Even if, as a leader, you believe yourself to have the intelligence and skill set that places you above your employees, that attitude must be tempered and replaced by a humble example, demonstrating that the rules and regulations apply equally to everyone on the team if you are to be successful.

Humility means knowing your limitations. Prior to starting this project, I reached out to people in various career fields to get their views on leadership. Friends, associates, and acquaintances who worked as military officers, special operations personnel, journalists, former CEOs, schoolteachers, and pastors all offered up similar principles, with a key principle always tying itself to humility. A gentleman from my high school who is now an accomplished navy officer offered one of the most astute assessments of anyone: "A leader doesn't have to be the smartest person in the group, or the fastest. As a matter of fact, any leaders surround themselves with people that are smarter than themselves. You cannot, however, be inept. You have to have sufficient knowledge and skills to have the respect of your troops."

While there are many different principles this statement can fall under while retaining the same effectiveness, I like to find a twist of humility in it. Are you, as a leader, humble enough to share the spotlight with people who may be smarter than you? Are you, as a leader, humble enough to admit that you don't know everything about everything? If so, you are already working at building a successful team. However, as my friend acknowledged, you cannot be inept. This means you must possess a working knowledge of everything that you are overseeing, or else you will be inefficient and ineffective with your decision making.

## Service

Service is also a characteristic that displays humility by example. This could even be considered a characteristic relating to integrity. Service does not necessarily have to be service in your immediate working environment; rather, it can be something accomplished in your personal life that makes those you lead take notice of your character. How do you spend your free time? Do you come to work talking about things you've done that impacted only you, or do you come to work telling a story of how you helped someone else? Service toward others should always be voluntary. This humbling act demonstrates a character trait that will make others take notice. It lets those around you and under you see that you placed others' needs ahead of your own. In turn people will be more willing to follow you when they believe that you have their best interests at heart.

Shortly after I finished my master's at seminary, I talked to a high school classmate whom I had not seen since graduation. He took a keen interest in what I'd done and what I intend to do, and he offered tremendous insight about service with humility being an example. As I was discussing my ideas for providing service for the elderly and the homeless, I questioned whether or not social media could play a role in this without appearing self-aggrandizing. My biggest concern was to not appear as though I wanted a pat on the back for doing something good. He responded by recommending that I just share my activities in a humble manner and allow my actions to speak for themselves. He believed that social media could be a wonderful tool for demonstrating leadership by example, and so far he has been absolutely correct, as others have seen fit to begin volunteering to serve others in their own ways. You can never lead if you are never seen, but it is important to walk the fine line of humility, allowing your actions to be the deciding factor in having people follow you, as opposed to your words. This is a trait that applies to every walk of life, transcending family and impacting your leadership of others in business.

## Trust

Are you trustworthy? Do people understand beyond a shadow of a doubt that your word is truth? Not only is trustworthiness a characteristic of integrity, but it also arises again in accountability. Trust as a leader goes beyond honesty to include faith. Do you micromanage every detail from your leadership position? Is it bad to be a micromanager? If you feel the need to micromanage every detail, then you have no trust in those working for you. The micromanager not only displays distrust but also takes on an overbearing load, which makes the primary responsibility much more difficult. The micromanager is also assuming the persona of the person who knows everything about everything, refusing to surround himself with people smarter than he is and inevitably displaying the areas in which he is weakest.

A good leader will know when to delegate responsibilities and in this process of delegation will seek out others who display proper leadership principles. The worst leader is one who delegates the most responsibilities to those who will simply follow orders without any latitude for creative input. There are often times when a task requires on-the-fly thinking, and the latitude offered in a trusting relationship allows for the problem to be solved immediately.

How many times have you been involved with an organization where responsibilities are delegated but the parameters to operate are so strict that important decisions must often wait until someone else is available? This is not a trusting relationship. Unfortunately we tend to choose people similar to ourselves to delegate responsibilities to. I say "unfortunately" because even the most well-intentioned leaders who seek out people like themselves create a linear thought process in which no new innovative ideas will be offered. I also say "unfortunately" because many people struggle with some principle of leadership, opting to delegate to the person who will offer the least resistance to the order being issued. Such a person is known as a yes-man.

When delegating responsibilities to others, it is important to find someone with a superior knowledge of the area you are assigning him to. Not only will that area become stronger, but with trust in the delegate, the need to micromanage will disappear, lessening stress. This also offers an opportunity for the senior leader to gain more in-depth knowledge from someone more experienced. The general consensus is that a leader can effectively oversee only five to seven people; to stretch responsibility to more than that lessens the effectiveness in all areas. The act of delegation is also a sign of proper organization. An organized leader is a successful leader. If your office is a cluster of paperwork that must be rooted through, odds are your leadership will be a cluster as well. An organized office makes a visual impression to everyone you interact with that you have a plan and that your program will run as efficiently as your office. It is very easy to assume that these little things make no difference to the overall job, but this actually is an example that your delegates will buy into.

## Inspire and Challenge

"Carrots and sticks" is a euphemism for rewards and punishments. As a leader, which do you think would garner the best results? The answer is both; however, carrots should always weigh a little heavier. Successful businesses have a rewards system in place. Employees will always view this as inspirational for doing a better job. If employees are challenged to hit a certain objective, knowing that there is a reward at the end, the quality of work increases significantly even if the quantity does not. This is being invested in your job. Rewards are a difficult concept for the fiscally conscious manager because on the surface the only constant he has to judge by is the value of the reward. Sometimes it takes a leap of faith to realize that the end is worth the means.

I like to view "carrots" and "sticks" as two simple words that subordinates will translate. When an employee hears "If you do this, then you will get this," he will realize that there is a reward at stake for the quality of work he does. On the contrary, when an employee hears, "If you do *not* do this, then you will get this," the employee immediately feels as if he is not a valuable asset to the team but rather just a body filling a spot that anybody could fill. Employees are an asset, but they are the most important asset. If an employee feels he has no more value than the machinery he is working on, quality and quantity will suffer, turnover will be high, and the possibility of injury will rise. If an employee feels as if he is the most valuable asset, he will feel personally invested in the job that he does, leading to a high quantity, good quality, worker stability, and a safe work environment. If you are in a position of leadership, which of these methods do you operate under?

### Value

Both of the above methods indicate value. Outside of traditional compensation, what is the true value of your employees? What do your employees feel their value is? Obviously all employees feel as if their value is more than it actually is. So how can we quantify value in ways other than direct cash compensation? The answer is simple; it is in how an employee feels he is treated. This does not mean that all employees should be treated according to the buddy system, where the impression is left that the leader and the subordinate are equals.

Not all jobs operate in a manner where senior leadership and low-level employees can allow hierarchy to be informal. In jobs that require close-knit teamwork, such as first responders or military personnel in specialized units, there is a mutual respect and admiration among teammates. In these situations, where equal training, equal rewards, and equal opportunity for loss exist, chain of command is recognized, appreciated, and followed while working. Off the clock, however, the brotherhood or sisterhood developed within the unit allows for a close-knit relationship in which hierarchy is secondary to friendships.

These kinds of relationships are not feasible in jobs where various levels of education, training, and rewards are present. In these types of situations, the hierarchy must be clearly defined and adhered to; if not, friendly gestures can be easily misinterpreted as favoritism among those in the workplace. This is counterproductive. This type of value shown to employees is inefficient but can be replaced easily with three simple methods to boost employee morale and team building.

The first method a good leader will employ to demonstrate value to his employees is listening. "Leaders must listen. It gets passed over, and just because you're in charge doesn't mean you have all the answers. Subordinates often have some great ideas if you take the time to listen." These words were offered by a former member of the US Army's elite Delta Force. As an associate in a civilian professional membership organization, I know this man practices what he preaches. He often leads training evolutions, and he is quick to respond to any questions. While the vast majority of civilian businesses are not structured with as much formality as the military, isn't it interesting that two military leaders, from two different backgrounds and branches, both made similar assessments of the importance of knowledge in subordinates? The first I included in the section on humility, though it was given to me as relating to being proficient, and this one pertains to the concept of listening.

Why does it seem so difficult sometimes in civilian business practices for people in leadership to put aside their egos and recognize the value of their subordinates? In theory, it should be simpler in the civilian world—owing to the variety of education, training, and backgrounds of coworkers—to recognize that there may be better ways and ideas of accomplishing a task. Perhaps this is part of the problem. In the civilian world, a coworker seen with more knowledge in a particular area becomes much more threatening to the person holding the leadership position than in the military's formal structure.

Insecurities must be put aside if the goal is to foster teamwork and build a successful business in which product is the end result. The ability to listen and be accepting of other ways and methods offered by employees is a very simple way to show an employee value. Once again the employee is invested in his job and feels the satisfaction that transcends a paycheck. Almost everyone has probably encountered a leader that was demoralizing because he refused to listen. If you have encountered a leader like this, think of how this impacted your performance.

The second method used to demonstrate value to an employee is enabling. A good leader will recognize each employee as an important asset to the business. As such, it is in the best interest of the business to ensure each employee is put in the best position to succeed. Enabling an employee is a very simple process, because all that is required is employing principles I have already discussed. As leaders, if we have done our due diligence in listening to our employees, we will be well aware of what it takes to meet particular needs.

In meeting these particular needs, an additional strength is required of the leader, and that is the ability to remove any obstacles standing in the way of an employee's success. If, as a leader, you have inspired and challenged your employee; if you have trusted and valued your employee; and if you have removed the obstacles you learned of by listening to your employee, then you have put your employee on the path to succeed at his particular task. Enabling in essence becomes the application of the aforementioned processes. This is something that should be easy and natural to implement—making a task easier and providing a sense of value that not only were the voices of those at the bottom heard but also that results were achieved.

The third method of showing value to your employees is also extremely easy to implement at this stage, and that is empathizing. The display of empathy toward your employees is an incredible value enhancer, as when you show empathy, your employees know you care. We have all heard the sayings "talk is cheap" and "actions speak louder than words," but what makes empathy so special is that it requires the person in a leadership position to appear to go out of his way for one particular employee. Many of the previously mentioned principles, when enacted, make empathy second nature.

As the leader, you have demonstrated your core values and integrity through your example. You have been humble by not accepting credit and taking all of the blame, while displaying the principles of trust to those around you. If trustworthiness and humility are to be taken seriously and not merely as an act of show, the empathy toward your employees by empowering them to be invested in the business through rewards, as well as listening and enabling them to be the best they can be, will create a culture your employees will look forward to coming to work in.

## Know Your Strengths

One of the hardest things for people to do is to admit their weaknesses, but being a successful leader requires just that. We have established the importance of surrounding yourself with capable people through delegation. These are people who have particular strengths and who may be more knowledgeable in some aspects than the leader. Much of this has already been dealt with in previous sections, but it is a principle important enough to be mentioned once more. Many times in the workforce, a person in charge is fearful of admitting his weaknesses, not only out of a sense of pride but also out of a fear that he may be replaced in his position by someone more knowledgeable and perhaps more capable. In reality, those who put up the biggest fronts are oftentimes the ones who lack the most confidence. A confident leader is secure in his position and understands that by surrounding himself with people who are stronger in certain areas, the team and the business will benefit as a whole.

Business, like a team sport, relies on the person in charge to put each individual into a position where he can flourish. Sometimes as leaders we must treat ourselves the same way. Think of a football team that utilizes a third-down back. Why is this player called a third-down back? This is an individual whose strengths generally include having good hands for catching passes and the quickness necessary to gain a first down. At the same time, this individual is probably a little bit undersized for rushing the ball on first or second down. The coach must realize the strengths of this one individual and how he can best benefit the team. The player meanwhile must accept what his role is and understand that if he succeeds in this role, then the team wins.

The first class I had to take in seminary was one that required a lot of introspection, the idea being that if someone was in a pastoral role and could not be humble enough to admit his own weaknesses, he would never be able to help others in the manner they deserved. This introspection went even deeper than an individual merely admitting strengths and weaknesses; it also included the much harsher reality of being told what one's weaknesses are and then accepting them. This was an assignment based on interviewing a spouse or close family member who knew the student very well. The first half of the questionnaire was very simple because it tended to boost the ego through questions that required the interviewee to describe the student's strengths, and honestly, who does not want to hear someone he loves and respects tell him all these wonderful things? Every coin has two sides, however, and the last half of the questionnaire dealt with weaknesses. It is one thing to admit to yourself deep down inside that you have areas of weakness and you do your best to cover them up. It is quite different, and difficult, to hear a loved one tell you the weaknesses he perceives.

We do not always do a very good job of covering our weaknesses, which is why it is so fundamentally important that we own our weaknesses. Unless we are able to openly admit the areas in which we are deficient, we will never seek out those people who can turn those deficiencies into strengths. In this way, a leader is constantly seeking self-improvement. Education comes in many forms, and there is nothing wrong with delegating an area of your weakness to someone who possesses that area as a strength and then watching and learning.

## *Theological Significance*

As important as accountability is in the professional world, accountability in the personal world holds even more significance, as the consequences are much greater. From the perspective of a religious person, accountability can be the difference between eternal life and eternal punishment. Those results are obviously much longer lasting than a business that succeeds or fails. Ownership takes on a much bigger context as it relates to religion, because God always knows the truth.

Every religion asks that you try to live the life of the religion's founder. In Christianity, we are tasked with emulating the life of Jesus Christ. Of course, as mortal humans, it is impossible to come close to the standard that he set. Rather, we must do our best to follow in the footsteps of His example. The Holy Bible is an incredible book for someone looking for examples both good and bad. There are examples of faith and righteousness, integrity and humility, service and empathy, and everything man needs to live a rewarding successful life. At the same time, we see the consequences of those who've done evil and failed to live up to the standards dictated by God. These are also examples of what not to do.

There are many passages in scripture that discuss examples—some more popular and well-known than others. First Timothy 4:12 finds the apostle Paul encouraging his young protégé to live as an example for others: "Let no one despise your youth, but be an example to the believers in word, in conduct, in love, in spirit, in faith, in purity." Paul is making a very clear point to Timothy, and that point is that age is no excuse to not be an example for others. Many times as adults we get caught up in the fast pace we set in our lives and forget that there are always eyes upon us. Often they are the eyes of youth. Are we always conscious in our day-to-day activities that our conduct may influence someone impressionable? At the same time, are we cognizant to the actions of youth that may stand out as exemplary? There is a commonly used phrase that goes, "Oh to have the faith of a child." With age, unfortunately, comes a certain cynicism, and there are times when we need to view that faith of a child as an example we can follow in our own lives.

It is not enough that we follow an example and set an example; we sometimes must take a step back and understand the sacrifice that goes into the example we are studying. Sacrifice is a tremendous example of the kind of character we should try to live our lives with. Television, movies, books, and newspapers often tell stories of sacrifice. Sometimes the sacrifice may be small, while other times the sacrifice is as great as giving up a life. These are the times we sit back and look at ourselves and say, "Do I have what it takes to make that kind of a sacrifice?" Obviously not everyone is expected to go out and sacrifice his own life, but it should add perspective to what leading by example means.

The greatest sacrifice in Christianity is the whole reason for Christianity, and that is the sacrifice of Jesus, carrying the burden of sin for all mankind, on a Roman cross. The apostles understood this sacrifice first, and the example set by Jesus was the core tenet of their teachings. The apostles did not want to be honored and worshipped; rather, they wanted to teach not only with their words but also by the examples of their lives while always giving credit to the sacrifice of Jesus. "Therefore take heed to yourselves and to all the flock, among which the Holy Spirit has made you overseers, to shepherd the church of God *He purchased with His own blood*" (Acts 20:28).

As adults, we should recognize it is impossible to live a perfect life and set a perfect example, but if we live according to the core values we set for ourselves and our families, we will lay a very solid foundation on which we can build. Sometimes living as a good example requires conditioning, because we are often oblivious that someone is always watching us. First thing in the morning, we need to make a conscious effort to find one particular area we can focus on for the day. After a few days and weeks of being conscious of the example we are living, it will become second nature. It is very easy to assume that we are good leaders and setting a good example because we are happy with where we are in life, but the standards we set for ourselves are not always applicable to others. If we are conscious as to how we can improve a little bit every day, we are taking accountability for our example.

## Humility

> Therefore if there is any consolation in Christ, if any comfort of love, if any fellowship of the spirit, if any affection and mercy, fulfill my joy by being likeminded, having the same love, being of one accord, of one mind. **let nothing be done through selfish ambition or conceit,** but in lowliness of mind let each esteem others better than himself. Let each of you look out not only for his own interests, but also for the interests of others. Let this mind be in

you which was also in Christ Jesus, who, being in the form of God, did not consider it robbery to be equal with God, but made himself of no reputation, taking the form of a bondservant, and coming in the likeness of men. And being found in appearance as a man, He **humbled** Himself and became obedient to the point of death, even the death of the cross. (Philippians 2:1–8)

For someone living within the Christian faith, is there a better example of humility? As we strive to live lives that serve as an examples for others, we often find ourselves in tugs-of-war. Everyone wants recognition. Everyone looks forward to a pat on the back. Even in our humility, we occasionally look forward to someone rewarding us for being humble! These are the times when we walk the fine line between self-promoting our humility and being seen setting an example of all the goodness that can be achieved through humility. Social media can often serve as a double-edged sword in this capacity. To the people who know us best, we are merely sharing what we are doing so they can share in our joy. To the people who may not know us so well, the appearance can sometimes seem self-aggrandizing.

What makes humility special is that it runs contrary to the famous American idea of "keeping up with the Joneses." One area of contention in modern society is the display of the Ten Commandments on government property. Why is this such an issue in a country founded on Judeo-Christian values? There are some misinterpretations in some Christian denominations that the Ten Commandments belonged to the old law of the Old Testament. Mainly these misinterpretations are found in congregations who choose to believe that the New Testament completely replaced what is found in the Old Testament. In twenty-first-century America, we see too many Christian denominations blatantly going against Christian laws in order to appease congregations that have become culturally corrupt. What we see in the Ten Commandments is a foundation for humility. The tenth commandment, which says, "You shall not covet your neighbor's house; you shall not covet your neighbor's wife, nor his male servant, nor his female servant, nor his ox, nor his donkey, nor anything that is your neighbors" (Exodus 20:17), can be translated into a caution against the modern-day saying, "I wish I had *that*."

There is no humility in desiring more than you need. For some, the biggest house, the flashiest car, or a trophy spouse is merely a way to draw the attention of others and to hear them say, "Boy are you lucky. I wish I had your life." This is the financial pat on the back and ego stroke that so many people define as success. Jesus rode into Jerusalem on a donkey as a lowly servant to set an example. Had He entered Jerusalem in a manner truly fitting His nature, He would have had the most expensive robes, a golden crown, and the most elaborate chariot, with the grandest stallions pulling it, accompanied by angels heralding with trumpets. But that was not His mission during His first coming. His mission was to set an example of how to humbly serve others. In Matthew 6:24, while addressing the multitude, Jesus said, "No one can serve two masters; for either he will hate the one and love the other, or else he will be loyal to the one and despise the other. You cannot serve God and mammon [money]." Which example do we choose to follow in our lives? Do we ground our roots of leadership in humility, or do we subtly boast with our wealth?

## Service

I do not believe there could be a more important characteristic of example and accountability with regard to theological significance than service. If examples of service were to be taken out of the Bible, we would have no Bible. Judeo-Christian ethics are theoretically based on service. The Old Testament prophets and the New Testament apostles served God *and* the people. From Adam, Enoch,

Noah, and Abraham to Peter, John, and Paul, the message of scripture is to be accountable to God through faith and service. This service went beyond performing holy rituals, to include teaching and demonstration. While the people during the time of the prophets were notorious for having hard hearts and not listening to what they were being told, the prophets still had to live their lives by example. If they did not practice what they preached, how could they expect anyone else to?

In order for service to be truly successful, it must be done voluntarily. We live in a world that seems enamored with mandating service and social justice, but the gains of that service are shallow, unfulfilling, and insignificant because they are achieved through force. True service is best reflected in free will. When Christianity sprang from the root of Judaism, free will became more important in society than before. Under the old laws, everyone in the society was expected to uphold the rituals and the teachings given to them by Moses. History has shown us that the society did not always succeed. The dawn of Christianity, however, allowed for all those in society to choose of their own volition whether or not to be believers. Free will is the basis on which voluntary service has meaning for setting an example.

In the story of the Good Samaritan, there was no mandate for people to stop and help; rather, it was the generosity, compassion, and humility of an individual from a race deemed unworthy that saved an innocent's life and set an example through service. There is, unfortunately, a mistaken notion that everyone who passes away will be in heaven. That idea is certainly comforting for those who've not embrace the faith of Christianity. As with every religion, there is a doctrine in Christianity that must be adhered to in order to reap rewards, and anything short of adherence brings judgment. This is the necessity of free will in the Christian doctrine, for if all were to reap the rewards, no matter the lives that they led, then the crucifixion would be meaningless.

God, as Father, is no different from any human parent that sets certain guidelines that children must obey lest they face punishment. If human parents allowed their children to do whatever they wanted whenever they wanted to do it, what would happen to the family? There would be anarchy and chaos within the family, as the children would be uncontrollable. God is no different. He issued us a set of guidelines to follow and came to earth as a man in order to face the same temptations and desires that mankind does, for only in that manner could man never argue that a righteous God is judging unfairly because He cannot relate to man. Instead God is able to judge righteously because He faced the same trials and temptations that man does by living as a man, by humbling himself as a servant, by living as an example, and by displaying leadership that has been followed by millions over two thousand years. The only caveat to gaining a heavenly eternity lies in the free will of acceptance—not in a mandate of social equality. Is there a more selfless display of service than this?

Let's briefly touch on a few passages of scripture detailing service. The first is from 1 Peter 5:2–4; in this passage, Peter is relaying to the new church elders what is expected of them; "Shepherd the flock of God which is among you, serving as overseers, not by compulsion but willingly, not for dishonest gain but eagerly; nor as being lords over those entrusted to you, but being examples to the flock." While this passage refers to what is expected of church leadership, it should also serve as an example of how every person should deal with others. Lead those among you willingly, not forcefully. Lead them not so you can get something out of it or serve as a master over them, but to be an example that they might follow in their lives and with those around them. Leadership is in willing service.

The next two passages take place during the Last Supper and serve as teachable moments as Jesus explains to his disciples what is expected of them. The first comes from Luke 22:24–27:

Now there was also a dispute among them as to which of them should be considered the greatest. And he said to them, "The kings of the Gentiles exercise lordship over them, and those who exercise authority over them are called benefactors. But not so among you; on the contrary, he who is greatest among you, let him be as the younger, and he who governs as he who serves. For who is greater, he who sits at the table, or he who serves? Is it not he who sits at the table? Yet I am among you as the One who serves."

At this time the disciples were suffering from a case of self-inflicted ego, each one wanting to be considered a greater disciple than the others. Jesus once again humbled himself in a service role, to lead by example, and taught an important lesson to his closest followers. In today's world, we have given a different word to what Jesus often does to those he is speaking to, and that is "shaming." We often see this on social media when someone takes a picture of his child holding a sign or places a sign around a pet's neck highlighting what the child or pet did wrong. We can look at some of these pictures and laugh at the comedic value they have, but Jesus uses a subtle, compassionate method for laying the lesson at his audience's feet.

The final passage we will look at concerning service is probably one of the most well-known stories pertaining to the Last Supper.

So when He had washed their feet, taken His garments, and sat down again, He said to them, "Do you know what I have done to you? You call me Teacher and Lord, and you say well, for so I am. If I then, your Lord and Teacher have washed your feet, you also ought to wash one another's feet. For I have given you an example that you should do as I have done to you. Most assuredly, I say to you, a servant is not greater than his master, nor is he who is sent greater than he who sent him." (John 13:12–16)

I believe this passage is self-explanatory, serving as a perfect indication that to serve others with humility sets the best example for those around you.

## Responsibility

What is the importance of responsibility in setting an example for leadership? Every adult knows what responsibility is, although it is questionable as to whether all adults embrace the concept. Many people find themselves in hardships and work diligently to overcome them, while some people hit a string of bad luck and expect to be bailed out by someone else. Those doing the bailing are usually heard saying that these people need to take responsibility over their lives. Responsibility seems as if it would be an easy concept to grasp, but like any other lesson, responsibility needs to be learned. We are not born into this world with an innate sense of responsibility. It is not an instinct ingrained in our DNA, nor is it something that we can teach ourselves. Those who are responsible are only so because they had an example, whether it was a good example or a bad example. How does a bad example teach responsibility? Look at the child who grows up in a home with an irresponsible parent. That child can go in one of two directions; either the child will also be irresponsible based on the easy-to-see example or that child will swear to himself that he will be different when he raises his own children.

Responsibility is one characteristic in others that is very easy to identify. When we see someone whose life is not going down a very good path, we can easily assume that he is not making very responsible decisions. When we see someone who is extremely organized, with many activities going on and his priorities in order, it is very easy to say that person is responsible. In most cases, being responsible is a reflection on core values, where we must stand for something. The responsible person always stands for something, and it is these convictions that motivate and drive one to be the best that he can be. If the old saying "Someone who stands for nothing will fall for anything" is valid, then it should align with the irresponsible person continually making bad choices. Oftentimes it does.

Which example do you wish to set? Since we are always being viewed by others, our reputations are irrevocably tied to the choices we make. The parent whose child is often in trouble, has no curfew, and engages in bad habits while underage quickly gathers a reputation in the community as being an irresponsible parent. This is typically a case in which perception is reality, and until changes are viewed outwardly, nothing the parent does at home will change that reputation. As adults we are tasked not only with leading our own children but also with serving as role models to all of the youth we engage with. Leadership in our communities must begin with our leadership at home, and the appearance of responsibility is invaluable.

All of this may seem more like common sense than theology, but there are biblical principles at work. For example let's see what Matthew 24:45–47 has to say on the matter. "Who then is a faithful and wise servant, whom his master made ruler over his household, to give them food in due season? Blessed is that servant whom his master, when he comes, will find so doing. Assuredly, I say to you that he will make him ruler over all his goods." This lesson from Jesus teaches us that even in the service of others, if we do our duties diligently and responsibly, we will be blessed with rewards. For those who know the story of Joseph from the Old Testament, do Jesus' words sound familiar? Joseph was sold into bondage by his brothers out of jealousy, and during Joseph's time as a slave in Egypt, his faithfulness to God enabled everything Joseph touched to flourish. As Joseph's works continued to flourish, he was given more responsibility over his master's home.

Throughout the trials and tribulations that Joseph endured, even as the de facto lord of his master's manor, Joseph's faithfulness and responsibility eventually gained him the governorship of Egypt. The pharaoh declared himself greater than Joseph in name only, and all of Egypt was to pay tribute to Joseph. This responsibility met its greatest test as Joseph stored seven years of grain during a time of plenty in order to endure seven years of famine. The rewards for Joseph were great indeed, as God then blessed him for his work by allowing him to save his father and his brothers and all of their families during the famine. Truly being responsible in one's service, and doing it humbly, sets a person apart. In this manner, we do indeed reap what we sow.

As we look at the final passage for our purpose, pertaining to responsibility, we will find another quote that has made its way into popular usage. Luke 12:42–44, 48 reiterates what was in Matthew regarding serving a master.

> And the Lord said, "who then is that faithful and wise steward, whom his master will make ruler over his household, to give them their portion of food in due season? Blessed is that servant whom his master will find so doing when he comes. Truly, I say to you that he will make him ruler over all that he has. …
> But he who did not know, yet committed these things deserving of stripes, shall be beaten with few. **For everyone to whom much is given, from him much will be required; and to whom much has been committed, of him they will ask the more.**"

Those who have been blessed through their responsible actions will be required to use their examples to teach others the proper way to conduct themselves. If they are rewarded but do not extend their lessons to others in service, why should they continue to be rewarded?

To be responsible is to be accountable. With responsibility comes respect. As role models, we have a primary responsibility to our youth; and with that responsibility, we must always offer credit when they do something well. If the youth we are tasked with mentoring do not meet the standard we have set, we must first look at ourselves to see why. Most likely we failed in explaining what our expectations actually were; therefore, offering punishments to someone who did his best without fully understanding what he was to do would be unjust. There is a significant difference between blatant disregard and disobedience, and misunderstanding. Before we react, we must determine which has happened. If the result is that we were irresponsible in relaying our expectations, we must own that error and take full blame as responsible role models. Our accountability always goes beyond ourselves.

### Trust

In the year 2016, trust is one of the most difficult principles to embrace. We turn on the evening news, open a website or a newspaper, and we are inundated with bad news. Terrorism, mass shootings, robberies, and rapes happen in places we used to think were safe. How can we reconcile these terrible events with the ability to have trust? We must start by realizing what we can control and what we cannot, and then we begin to build our inner sanctum, gradually extending it outward to the strangers we come face-to-face with.

Trust is everywhere in the Bible. Every character in the Bible who had a relationship with God had an unwavering trust in God. "Trust" is sometimes used as a synonym for "faith"; however, they are quite different. Faith is something we have, while trust is something we do. In essence, trust is faith in action. To quote Nolan Dalla, "Faith has been called the 'substance of hope.' It requires no evidence for belief or practice. The very nature of faith surmises the tangible evidence doesn't exist. Otherwise, there is manifestation. On the other hand, trust is based largely on evidence that is real. Trust is the core conviction of judgment based on knowledge, instinct, and experience."[10] While I tend to strongly disagree with how Mr. Dalla disregards the principle of faith throughout the rest of his article, his statement works perfectly for describing trust among the faithful to God.

Those from the Bible who set examples by living in faith had unwavering trust in God because they saw the beauty in His rewards. For them, what started out as substance of hope quickly turned into evidence that was real, cementing their core conviction of trust, which was truly based on knowledge, instinct, and experiences. Essentially trust became an offshoot of faith, and the more rewards they saw, the stronger their trust grew. Don't we go through the same types of experiences as we learn to trust? "Trust in the Lord with all your heart and lean not on your own understanding; in all your ways submit to Him, and He will make your paths straight" (Proverbs 3:5–6 NIV).

While we cannot expect other people to submit to us, we can learn to trust in others. Stubbornness that shows itself in the workplace also shows itself among our family and friends. We tend to lean on our own understanding without giving any credence to how somebody else approaches a problem. There are generally many ways to solve a problem, and we must learn to be open-minded enough to trust that those around us have the best of intentions. It is also true that trust is the hardest thing to regain once it has been lost. We can become skeptical after we have been through disappointment, and place our now unfounded fears upon an innocent person.

I believe that the idea of trust is very difficult for most people, as everyone has been through some form of disappointment. Friends and family are not a business, and we cannot treat them with the same rigidity we would use if we were searching for a better bottom line. This area is constantly a work in progress for me as well. One time in a business environment, a superior remarked that I was too

---

[10] Nolan Dalla, "The Difference Between Faith and Trust," NolanDalla.com, May 19, 2014, http://www.nolandalla.com//?s=trust+and+faith&x=0&y=0.

hard on someone for the way he did something, because there was more than one way to do it. I replied by stating that his remark was true, as there are three ways to do something: the wrong way, the inefficient right way, and the efficient right way. When it comes to personal relationships, though, efficiency is never the issue. With personal relationships, what is most important is to help someone to grow as an individual by walking the right path and trusting in him to follow the example you set.

## Delegation

Delegation is not necessarily a major issue in the realm of developing personal relationships, but whenever trust is involved, a certain amount of delegation must be involved as well. As we strive to set examples for others, we must make sure that those who are following our lead are capable of leading others in the proper way. It is then important to begin delegating small tasks of leadership that individuals can begin to gradually employ in leading others. In the Bible, delegation is God's tool for communicating with His people. The prophets were delegated their positions—some unwillingly, such as Jeremiah—and they all fulfilled the obligation God set before them.

The book of Isaiah contains several chapters toward the end of the book that are considered by many Christian scholars to be the gospel of the Old Testament, and Isaiah's commissioning in chapter six shows God delegating authority to Isaiah face-to-face: "Also, I heard the voice of the Lord, saying: 'Whom shall I send, and who will go for Us?' Then I said, 'Here am I! Send me.' And He said, 'Go, and tell this people: ... '" The appointment of Isaiah to do God's bidding came at a crucial time for the Northern and Southern Kingdoms of Israel and Judah. God needed a strong voice, and He even warned him in advance that the people would not listen; but something about Isaiah made him the right man for the job, and God delegated that work.

Of course, Isaiah is not the only one to be commissioned face-to-face by God and have a mission clearly delegated. In the New Testament, following the resurrection, Jesus gave a commission to His disciples as well: "And He said to them, 'Go into all the world and preach the gospel to every creature. He who believes and is baptized will be saved; but he who does not believe will be condemned'" (Mark 16:15–16). In Christianity, this is what is known as the Great Commission. This is the duty that has been delegated to all followers of Christ throughout history. The disciples understood and obeyed, converting thousands before each met an untimely death. Through the example of leadership, they taught as they were taught, with the understanding that those who have been saved are tasked with the same commission Jesus assigned to them.

In today's world of turmoil, religious wars, cultural degradation, and general ambiguity, even some of the most personally responsible Christians fail to heed their delegated tasks. It is so simple to worry only about ourselves, but in that process we are failing miserably at fulfilling the mission God has delegated to us. As we live out our normal days and we do our best to lead by example, and trust in those around us, we must also make sure others are prepared to go forth with the mission we are each leading. Family, friends, coworkers, and even the stranger at the end of the off-ramp are waiting for someone to lead them into happier times. Those times come when we are working toward a greater purpose. Give someone a simple job, and with faith and trust, you will be amazed at what he can do with it. Delegation is the only way to successfully reach others outside your immediate circle. Jesus understood this, and we must follow this.

### Inspire

In religious circles, inspiration is the easiest task to achieve. Seminary students are taught that it is not necessary to fight the whole battle of converting someone to faith in Jesus. Merely plant the seeds and allow the Holy Spirit to provide the water. For those who have found themselves living in a gray area in which things do not always go their way, if they are not ready to give up their faith, it is sometimes a random speaker on television or in church that takes over their hearts. This newfound burst of energy provides the inspiration they need to begin reading scripture again, to begin serving others again, and to begin living life to its fullest again. Inspiration comes from unlikely sources, but it is always the work of the Holy Spirit. The same inspiration is not effective for everyone. Each individual responds differently to the stimuli placed in front of him. If, as leaders, we take a cookie-cutter approach to inspiration, then many people will be left feeling unfulfilled. To be legitimate leaders, we must take an interest in each individual. It is our responsibility to find out what motivates those around us and under us. In order for us to trust those we have delegated responsibility to, it is essential that we know the types of people we are dealing with. Do we wish to put responsibility that ultimately falls back onto us into the hands of strangers? By knowing people, we will learn what motivates them, allowing us to tailor our message to provide the best possible inspiration for each individual.

If there are two individuals in your life and each is tasked with fulfilling a certain obligation for you in order to reach others, but each has a different strength, how do you inspire them to reach the same goal? For instance, perhaps one person is very strong at oral communication, while the other is not a very good speaker but an excellent writer. Each is to provide a missionary outreach to a group of people in order to spread the word of God. You are tasked with setting up the best method to achieve that outreach. Obviously you want the powerful speaker to be in front of a group of people, using his charisma to spark life into others. The writer, meanwhile, is best suited to presenting a short written program that will captivate a reader's imagination. These two individuals are attempting to achieve the same goal with different strengths. Our task, then, is to find a motivation that works effectively for each individual, allowing them both to do their best work.

We are tasked with being an example, having trust, delegating our work, and inspiring others to greatness. In Matthew 20:26–28, we witness Jesus doing all this for His disciples: "Yet it shall not be so among you; and whoever desires to become great among you, let him be your servant. And whoever desires to be first among you, let him be your slave, just as the Son of Man did not come to be served, but to serve, and to give His life as a ransom for many." Jesus was and is the perfect example that all believers must attempt to emulate. He trusts that His disciples will carry out their mission. He delegates the work He expects them to carry out, and He inspired his followers by saying, "just as the Son of Man," demonstrating to his disciples that he expects them to do the same type of work He did in the same fashion He did it. How could that not be inspiring? Jesus Himself is telling his followers, "This is what I do, and you can do it too!"

We can inspire our children by not inhibiting their passions. If your children are musical, surround them with instruments. If your children are artistic, give them paper and paints. If your children are athletic, give them the proper equipment. If your children are scholarly, ensure they have access to books. The worst thing we can do to our children is smother their passions and marginalize their dreams because we feel they do not meet our standards. We can inspire our friends in the same manner. If your friend has a dream or a goal, do not be the person who puts a wet blanket on that creativity. Offer constructive advice and use whatever resources are available to you to help your friend find fulfillment in his dreams. Inspiration can be as simple as enabling someone to be the best he can be.

## Challenge

One question I frequently ask myself is, why do people give up so easily? It is painful to see the potential in people and realize they do not see it in themselves. Why? Too often people get complacent in life and forget they once had dreams. Perhaps they tried once or twice in the past and failed, and they just can't take the beating of failing again. Perhaps they have never even tried because they were never encouraged to do so. Are we successful friends and parents if we do not challenge those we care the most about to reach their potential?

In order to achieve dreams, we must put forth a lot of work. If a lot of work were not necessary, then everyone would be living out his dream today. Yet it is obvious when we talk to other people that there is so much more they would like to do. The good Lord put us on this earth for a finite period of time and proceeded to surround us with an infinite amount of opportunities to experience. He did this so we may live our lives to the fullest. We must always embrace the things around us and use them to drive us forward. It is disturbing to speak with elderly people and hear them say, "I wish I would have done this." When you are young, it is very easy to fall into a trap of thinking you have all the time in the world; before you know it, you are looking back at life, wishing you would have at least tried to fulfill your dreams. Sometimes we realize that we can go only so far on our own and that occasionally we need someone else to help pull us over the top.

To challenge someone to fulfill his dreams requires a push/pull effort. It is very easy to stand on the side and push someone along by simply telling him that you believe in him. Oftentimes, pushing will take someone only so far. When a person has reached his limit and pushing will not take him any farther, it is necessary to pull him the rest of the way. For example, if someone were trying to scale a fifteen-foot wall and you were helping him by providing a push up, odds are they would still be short of being able to get over the top. This is a time when we need someone on the wall to offer a hand and say, "Give me your hand and let me help pull you up." The aspect of pushing is often easier than being the puller.

If we are successful in providing inspiration to those around us, then we have helped foster the mentality for achieving dreams. Are we successful if we stop there? How many times in your life have you seen someone quit, or never even try, because he could not believe in himself and no one else was there to help him? I believe everyone has had this experience at some time. Are you in a position to challenge your children and friends? This question can be answered relatively easily, because the answer lies in the example you set. Have you tried to fulfill your potential? Have you gone after your dreams? Do you believe that if you can't do it, then no one around you can either? If this is the case, then perhaps you view contentment as fulfillment. Not everyone can be as easily placated. This is the time when you can step up and say, "Just because I wasn't able to do this does *not* mean that you cannot do this." You are now in a position to be a pusher. Present the challenge to your children and friends that they can do whatever they set their minds to. Demonstrate faith in them, show you have trust in them, and be willing to be there when you are needed to pick them up during tough times.

There are many biblical examples of times God issued challenges to his servants. Let's look at two big challenges God presented; had man quit and not overcome them, the world would be vastly different. The first involves our old friend Noah. Prior to Noah's day, the earth had never seen rain. Vegetation was watered from pools within the earth, and man merely had to dip out his drinking water. Corruption was rampant among man, as we remember from Genesis 6, and God was saddened that He had created man. He looked at Noah and saw righteousness, and He issued an unfathomable challenge to His servant. "Noah, I want you to build an ark." Noah undoubtedly said, "What's an ark, and what is this rain you are going to bring upon the earth?" In faith Noah accepted the challenge and built a boat; all the while, he was probably mocked by his peers. Over the years it took Noah to build this ark, he probably felt like quitting. He was a mortal man challenged to build something he had never heard of, for an event he had never experienced. What Noah had in his favor was the greatest pusher/puller there could be—God Himself. It was God who gave Noah the strength necessary to see his challenge through to the end and save mankind from extinction. Have you ever had a challenge as great as Noah's?

Another great example of someone stepping up to a challenge is Moses. Here is a man who grew up believing he was Egyptian royalty, with the throne of Egypt at his fingertips. He was being prepared to be the most powerful man in the world, and then God threw him a curveball. Moses was faced with the realization that he was not Egyptian royalty but rather the son of slaves, and he was cast out into the desert, where he was expected to perish. God had other ideas.

Oftentimes we look at the challenges we face in life and wonder how much more can we take. We think we have hit rock bottom when something else happens to drive us even lower. Little do we realize that the strongest steel is forged in the hottest fire. Moses wandered through the desert hungry and thirsty, and most likely waiting for death, not realizing that God was fashioning him, like a strong blade, to do His bidding and free His people. Try to imagine Moses, having grown up worshiping Egyptian deities, standing at the foot of the holy mountain, looking up into a burning bush, and approaching the presence of the Creator, God. To say that he was overwhelmed would probably be an understatement. "Insecure and unworthy" would probably be an accurate description of the way Moses felt when God issued the challenge to him. "Go back to Egypt, to the same people who wanted to kill you, and tell them to set all of their slaves free, because it is the will of God." How many people would take up *that* challenge?

Was Moses skeptical? The entire way back across the desert to Egypt, Moses was probably telling himself, "I can't do this," while God was in his corner, saying, "Not only *can* you do this, but you *will* do this." That is an inspiring presence that not only issued the challenge but also served as the pusher and the puller, giving Moses the strength he needed to see the challenge through to completion. If he had not been successful with that challenge, the Israelites may still be subjects of Pharaoh. The Jewish faith, and its offspring, Christianity, would never have been able to flourish. For the believers in our God, we certainly owe a debt of gratitude to Moses for accepting the gauntlet God threw down before him and for persevering through the most difficult times to find success.

Proverbs 11:14 says, "Where there is no counsel, the people fall; But in the multitude of counselors there is safety." Even the most goal-driven people can go only so far on their own. No matter how big your hopes and dreams may be, or how independent you think you are, at some point along the way, you must have a helping hand. Set your challenges. Embrace your goals. Love the process. At the same time, you are tasked with being the counsel for someone else. We are here to serve, and at the height of your greatest achievement you can humbly recognize that someone else served you. Remember this and repeat it for those around you.

### Value

> For I say, through the grace given to me, to everyone who is among you, not to think of himself more highly than he ought to think, but to think soberly, as God has dealt to each one a measure of faith. For as we have many members in one body, but all the numbers do not have the same function, so we, being many, are one body in Christ, and individually members of one another. Having then gifts differing according to the grace that is given to us, let us use them: if prophecy, let us prophecy in proportion to our faith; or ministry, let us use it in our ministering; he who teaches, in teaching; he who extorts, and exhortation; he who gives, with liberality; he who leads, with diligence; he who shows mercy, with cheerfulness. (Romans 12:3–8)

What does this passage of scripture tell us about value? Let us look at this passage through the analogy of basketball. On a basketball team, each position is critical to the success of the team as a whole. The point guard has a specific role, as do the shooting guard, small forward, power forward, and center. When one member of the team, regardless of position, values himself more than the sum of the pieces, the team will fail to function effectively as a unit. Even the superstar must humble himself enough to realize that he is a cog in the bigger machine. He cannot succeed on his own, and likewise, the team cannot succeed without him. In order to work effectively as part of the greater body of Christ, it is essential to embrace our roles and the positions God assigns to us.

How should we value one another? Many people suffer with the perception of feeling insignificant. Often people have great ideas but refuse to share them because they feel their opinions will not matter. Outside of the business world, the people we influence the most are our children and our friends. Should any of these people feel that they do not matter to you? The answer is obvious—of course they should not! So what is it we do to make the people closest to us feel insignificant? This answer is not something that we intentionally *do*; rather, it is what we *do not* do. There is a very common phrase that gets thrown around once something is lost that one is used to having, and that is "I really took him/her/it for granted."

The husband who comes home from work to a clean house, clean clothes, a hot meal, and well-behaved children studiously working on their homework can quickly come to accept this as the norm. In doing so, his expectations rise to the new normal while he unintentionally overlooks the amount of hard work his wife put into achieving this peaceful setting. While he inadvertently takes his wife for granted, her sense of value declines as a result of even the smallest lack of recognition.

For the wife who gets into a safe vehicle, looks out the window onto a well-manicured yard, has security in her home, is able to purchase all the necessities for the family without worry, and accepts her husband working twelve-hour days, this sense of well-being becomes her normal level of expectation. She inadvertently takes her husband's hard work for granted, lessening his sense of value as a result of even the smallest lack of recognition.

Of course, these two examples are not realistic in every household. These two examples are more from old-fashioned style families, where perhaps a single income is enough to provide for the family and traditional roles are fulfilled. In the modern day, many families wish that this was still the case; however, we are in a world where both parents need to work and both parents are responsible for everything related to the family. Regardless of what one's situation may be, expectations of normalcy will arise over time, and with that, spouses begin to take each other for granted while reducing their senses of value. Sadly this is most often inadvertent and unintentional. These are the times when the little things possess the most value and we have fallen into too big of a funk to realize the significance a small gesture can have in making your loved one feel valued.

How can we rectify this in our families? Until we are able to value our family members, we will never be able to truly value our relationships outside the home. It is very easy to fall into our ruts, but with very little effort, we cannot pull out ourselves or our loved ones. One thing that has been lost in our fast-paced world is a family dinner—a set period of time for husband, wife, and children to talk and, most importantly, listen.

We live in an era when single-parent homes are everywhere. This puts great time restrictions on the interactions we can have with our children and also forces us to carry heavy burdens. For the single parent, being able to stop for just a few minutes would be a treasure. Even during the long sought after "me time," there is still no one around to share your concerns with. In this case, the significant other or best friend must be willing to step up and step in to provide a release valve for the one you love. Opening that valve is as simple as listening. It is often too easy to lay our expectations upon those we care about without fully realizing what is going on in their lives, and the sacrifices they are making to try to bring happiness to everyone. We fight, we argue, and we say things we don't mean in the heat of the moment and often wish we could take back, and it all comes from a lack of communication. Sometimes we may not explain ourselves very well, and a lot of times we do not really listen to an explanation being offered. How can we find value in each other, and happiness together, without listening to each other's valid concerns?

Too often the harshest criticisms we feel occur when someone we love says, "You never listen to me," because deep down, in our inherent nature, we realize we are stealing value from someone we love. Why do we do this? Is it our human egos? Life is short, and time moves quickly, and then we find ourselves once again looking back and saying, "I wish I would have taken more time to just listen."

There is a great difference between the secular and theological significance of valuing people; business is business—not your life. Theologically and personally, the way we value those around us is significantly more important than it is in the business world. To devalue people in our personal lives ultimately leaves us very lonely. There is also a significant level of respect attached to the art of listening. Throughout the ministry of Jesus, He suffered from a lack of people listening, but probably nothing hurt his human spirit more than when those in his hometown would not listen.

After forty days in the wilderness, during which He was tempted by Satan, Jesus returned to his hometown of Nazareth, where He opened the book of Isaiah and read a prophecy pertaining to Himself. Closing the book, he declared that, "Today this Scripture is fulfilled in your hearing" (Luke 4:21). The townspeople, in awe, said, "Is this not Joseph's son?" (Luke 4:22). Jesus' reply is as relevant today as it was to Him at the time: "Assuredly, I say to you, no prophet is accepted in his own country" (Luke 4:24).

What is it about the statement that makes it relevant today? Unfortunately the people who know us the best or the longest oftentimes fail to see our growth as people, instead opting to view us as who we once were, which is extremely devaluing to an individual's growth. The townspeople of Nazareth saw Jesus as Joseph's son as opposed to the Son of God and the Messiah that Isaiah spoke of. How often have you tried to explain something to someone you are close to, only to have him look at you as if you are from another planet?

A personal story related to this comes from a time when I was giving scriptural interpretation to a couple of people extremely close to me. Their response was filled with stubbornness and a clear indication they were not listening to what I had to say. My only reply was to quote what Jesus said about the people of Nazareth. Had I been a stranger assigned to the pulpit of their local church or an evangelist speaking through the television, my words would have had more meaning and possibly contributed to further study of what the scripture actually said. Instead I walked away feeling hurt and devalued with the impression that my growth as a person and my ability to attain knowledge were insignificant to people whose opinions I valued so much. If we truly love those who are closest to us, we will do everything we can to provide them value, and that requires listening to all they have to offer with an open mind and an open heart. If we fail to do this for the people who are closest to us, how can we expect to be leaders of strangers? If we fail to remove our stubbornness, our egos, and our inclination to take things for granted, we will never grow into the potential God set before us. In order to be leaders, it is essential that we value others.

As previously mentioned, another method for valuing someone is enabling. This is most effective when dealing with your children. This ties back into inspiring and challenging when you provide your children the proper tools to be the best that they can be. It is shortsighted, however, to stop there; we must also verbally enable. Children must know that they have your full support as they pursue their dreams. A child should never be told "That's a dumb idea" or "I think that goal is unreachable." As we look back to the scriptural passage of Romans 12:3–8, which began the section on value, we must remember that people have various gifts. In humility we do not flaunt these gifts; however, they must be tenderly grown, like a flower. Just because as a parent you do not understand a particular gift, that does not mean the gift should be considered impossible.

The same applies to our friends. We must approach these relationships with realistic honesty yet not negativity. Those close to us should never feel that what they are attempting to do is impossible. Our purpose is to provide them with the proper tools and encouragement they need to make their dreams a reality. Have you ever had a friend come to you and state that they wish to start a business? Perhaps you have had a friend who has never displayed any athletic ability yet decided he wanted to run a marathon. How did you respond to your friend's statements? Did you provide some sort of support that would enable him to achieve his goals, or did you scoff and make him feel it was impossible?

If we value our friendships, then we wish to see our friends succeed as much as we wish to succeed ourselves. If you cannot be there for your friend in need, is it fair to expect your friend to be there for you when you need encouragement? We never know what is impossible unless we try. Despite the evil corruption in the world and the negativity that makes us feel we are constantly fighting an uphill battle, I continue to believe in the inherent goodness of man because that is how God created us. God enables our success by telling us to cast our worries upon Him. (See Psalm 55:22; 1 Peter 5:7.) It is our lack of faith that leads to our failures. Many people will respond to this by saying, "I prayed for help, but God ignored me," but there are two other possibilities. One is a lack of faith and belief in the God you prayed to. The other is that perhaps your will is not the path that God has designated for you to follow. As God requires our faith in order for us to be enabled, so to must our friends and loved ones have faith that we can help enable them to achieve their goals.

Empathy is generally much more difficult in the business world than in personal relationships. In personal relationships, we are dealing with people we love and care about. The end goal is not a better product or a higher quota; rather, it is the fulfillment of an individual's life that you cherish. Empathy is support, compassion, and love. Empathy in personal relationships is also sacrifice. We never wish to see a loved one struggle, and many times we hear people say, "If I could trade places with you, I would." Why do people say that? Because of our love and compassion, we are willing to take on the sacrifice necessary to ensure our friends and family recognize the value they have not only to us but also to the world. Empathy is the easiest way to value someone, as it requires nothing other than caring.

The ability to provide value to someone is so easily overlooked. Too many times we project our own thoughts and abilities onto those around us, and that is neither fair nor productive. Not everyone is the same. Each person's thought processes, talents, and potential are unique. Take a minute and ask yourself, "How well do I know my friends and family?" Have you given them your undivided attention? Have you truly listened to their cares and concerns? Have you done all you can to put them in a position to succeed? Have you offered your shoulder and your ear during their times of sadness? It is very easy to say that you love someone because he or she is a parent, a sibling, a child, or a friend, but having feelings of love and caring is not always enough to show someone how much you value his or her potential. Many times, your family and friends care very little for the opinions of the outside world if they believe *they* mean the world to you. God values us as His children and puts in front of us everything we need to be successful. Do we do the same for those we love?

Galatians 6:7–10 states, "Do not be deceived, God is not mocked; for whatever a man sows, that he will also reap. For he who sows to his flesh will of the flesh reap corruption, but he who sows of the Spirit will of the Spirit reap everlasting life. And let us not grow weary while doing good, for in due season we shall reap if we do not lose heart. Therefore, as we have opportunity, let us do good to all, especially to those who are of the household of faith."

Know your strengths, and in your strengths be humble and faithful, offering yourself as a servant to those in need. Place others before yourself and your value below that of others. In the end, your rewards will be greater when others are lifted up. Some may call this karma, but to the Christian, it is living in humility and service to others. Our value is in enriching others.

# KNOW YOUR PEOPLE

*Secular Significance*

By this time, anyone in a supervisory role should have a good idea about the people around him. This section is titled "Know Your People" because in essence it encapsulates everything discussed so far. If we have taken the time to incorporate our faith, vision, integrity, core values, and accountability into our place of business, we should not find ourselves surrounded by strangers. Rather, we should have a fairly intimate understanding of the strengths and weaknesses of everyone we are associating with. It is in this manner that our interpersonal relationships strongly come into play. We should have already weeded out those people who are hindrances to our goals, and now we are ready to move forward at full strength. With our strong team in place, the next important principle in our arsenal is to be able to effectively communicate.

Lack of effective communication is a leading cause of failure in the business environment. How many times throughout your work life have you encountered news coming through the grapevine that should have been delivered by your immediate superior? Unfortunately the answer is probably "Too many." Why do we fail to communicate? Communication is the basis of human interaction, yet the manner in which we communicate is often substandard. We have already discussed the importance of listening to those around us, and now we must take the lessons that we've learned from listening and effectively formulate a response that is understandable.

As leaders, if there is a misunderstanding, the onus falls upon us. We failed to clearly elaborate what our expectations were and the manner in which we expected them to be carried out. The bigger the business, the more important communication is. More departments means more people, and it becomes a heavy burden for the top manager to think he can micromanage multiple departments. In fact, the most effective communication is related to the trust you put in the people directly under you. It is virtually impossible to take on additional responsibilities without something suffering because one is stretched too thin. Do those directly under you have a thorough understanding of what the ultimate goals are, and have you reinforced the message?

Businesses frequently have staff meetings, and it is in these meetings that the plan and expectations are orally delivered. But is that enough? To ensure directions are concise and clear to all those involved, the oral presentation must be backed up with written directives. With something in writing, each person is able to clarify exactly what was intended in the meeting. At the departmental level, the same method should be used. Frequent notices on the bulletin board serve as a reference point and a reminder for all employees tasked with doing the job. At the same time, it is not enough to simply state, "This is what we're going to do." Employees are not children, and the simple answer parents usually give—"Because I said so"—is insufficient. In order for employees to buy into the plan, they must understand the rationale behind the plan, particularly if that plan is a change in direction away from what the employees are used to. Old ideas as well as old habits are difficult to break; therefore, employees must have an understanding as to why changes are being made. When the rationale is clearly articulated through proper communication, the employees are more likely to buy in and function as a tight-knit unit to ensure these new goals are met.

If you know your people, then communication should be easy, as you are aware of their tendencies, their motivations, and their individual goals. It is essential that we communicate effectively with each individual and never make assumptions that because we understand something, everybody should. Levels of education and experience play a vital role in how someone receives information. Not everyone in a traditional workplace has shared in the same level of training or in the same life experiences; therefore, the necessity of properly articulating the goals and expectations takes on critical importance.

Another principle that arises when you know your people is the way to effectively build your team. As we mentioned, not everyone has shared training or experiences; therefore, building an effective ground-floor team will require placing someone in his position of strength, where he is comfortable, capable, and able to contribute the most he can to the team's success. Only in specialized fields will a leader be fortunate enough to have a team that has equal levels of training and ability to fulfill every position on the team as required. In the traditional workplace, that is an unlikely luxury. The importance of building a successful team now relies on a supervisor's ability to intimately know the people under him.

Does every member of the team share the same goal? Has every member of the team bought into the plan? Is every member of the team fully capable of fulfilling his task? There are many businesses that possess the attitude that "any warm body will do." That is unfair to the team and unfair to the individual if he lacks the necessary requirements to be efficient and effective. Part of knowing your people requires a strong commitment to personally knowing the individuals. If the extent of the supervisor's knowledge of a potential employee goes only as far as a recommendation from someone else that the employee is strong at "such and such," and that employee fails, responsibility for the failure falls squarely on the supervisor who did not take the time or the effort to get to know the individual.

I once had a supervisor who was so invested in his employee's personal lives that he was aware of every ailment each person in his department suffered from. He would routinely take the time to ask how we were feeling, inquire as to whether there was anything that he could do to help, and ask about how our home lives were going. This supervisor recognized that baggage in his people would not be productive to the overall aims of the business. Knowing your people as you attempt to build a successful team can be as simple as listening and empathizing. What ultimately makes the team strong is a camaraderie based on knowing that the person beside you is proficient in his skill and dedicated to not letting down his teammates. In some ways the ability to build a team can be an art form.

Finally, having covered a few important principles of leadership, there is the ability to supervise. If all of the previous principles are effectively instituted, supervision is able to adequately blend leadership and management. Remember: at the beginning a very, important distinction was made between leadership and management. Not all good managers make good leaders, yet good leaders should make good managers. We have now reached the point where that statement is accurate. The most difficult part of the journey is often instituting principles that may be foreign to your lifestyle, but it is through these principles that a leader's character can truly shine. If you successfully demonstrate integrity, properly share your vision through solid communication, delegate authority to people that you trust, willingly accept accountability for everything under you, put forth the time and effort to know your people, and display unwavering faith that the decisions you make are for the best, then supervising as a leader is as simple as maintaining the parameters you have set forth.

*Theological Significance*

The ability to know your people from a theological perspective, given that thus far we have focused the theological perspective on leadership of family and friends, may seem like a silly concept. After all, they are *your* family and friends, so it should seem obvious that you would know them. However, knowing them does not mean that you effectively communicate with them, build them into a tight-knit team, or even provide supervisory leadership over areas at which they might be weak. Reflecting on previous statements, sometimes the better we think we know someone, the easier it is to take him for granted. By doing this, we do not necessarily put forth our best efforts to ensure the best chance of success.

In the Old Testament, a story exists in the book of Exodus pertaining to Moses and some sound advice he was given by his father-in-law, Jethro. At this time, Moses had just led the people out of Israel and was encamped at the foot of the holy mountain. Jethro was coming to meet Moses and bringing along Moses' wife and two sons, who were left in the safe care of Jethro when Moses went back to face Pharaoh. Jethro bore witness to Moses sitting from morning until evening, judging the people, and answering questions that were inquired of God. The advice Jethro offered to his son-in-law could be viewed as setting up the first corporation. Let's pick up the story from Exodus 18:17–22:

> So Moses' father-in-law said to him, 'The thing that you do is not good. Both you and these people who are with you will surely wear yourselves out. For this thing is too much for you; you are not able to perform it by yourself. Listen now to my voice; I will give you counsel, and God will be with you: stand before God for the people, so that you may bring the difficulties to God. And you shall teach them the statutes and the laws, and show them the

way in which they must walk in the work they must do. Moreover you shall select from all the people able men, such as fear God, men of truth, hating covetousness; and place such over them to be rulers of thousands, rulers of hundreds, rulers of fifties, and rulers of tens. And let them judge the people at all times. Then it will be that every great matter they shall bring to you, but every small matter they themselves shall judge. So it will be easier for you, for they will bear the burden with you.'

What Jethro effectively realized was that it is impossible for one man to oversee a great multitude and micromanage the activities of everyone. Jethro's advice was to trust in the abilities of others to effectively carry out God's plan. This message was effectively communicated to Moses and effectively communicated to each leader. How often do we find ourselves in situations where we are so busy that we are ineffective at managing and leading our households, or being there for our friends when we are needed? In the twenty-first century, everyone is busy all the time just to survive. When we become this self-absorbed in what we must do, what is the first thing that suffers when we are home? Our communication.

It is easy to become disengaged from the things that truly matter most, and that is what is happening with our families and our friends. When we become disengaged, although we "know" those close to us, we are unaware of the little details happening in their lives and what they really need from us. This unawareness leads us to communicate poorly. Sometimes our tone is too harsh, we choose words we later regret, or we opt to embrace silence just to find some peace in our own lives. Does this benefit the family unit? How can we rectify this problem? If we are successful in taking the time to listen in order to not take each other for granted, then we will learn what our loved ones are going through and be in a position to communicate properly. A favorite old saying of mine is, "Work to live, not live to work." How often we get the two confused. Work will always be there, but we have a limited amount of time to have a positive influence on our friends and families, and being aware of what is happening in their lives is something we can never get back if we miss out on it.

When we team build in our personal lives, we do it based on an intimacy that the whole is greater than the parts. Each of our families needs to be a team. We often choose our friends based on a shared moral code or on things we may have in common, and given such, we already have a foundation on which we can build our interpersonal team. What comes next is the time you are willing to put into your relationships. When we look at our lives, we probably all have an occurrence where we look at our friends and think to ourselves, "I have not been as good a friend to them as they are to me." Why do we feel that way? Are we allowing ourselves to be the weak link on the team? I am a firm believer that we are put into each other's lives to fulfill a purpose. That purpose may not necessarily be what we think it is, or even what we hope it may be, but it is something we must fulfill just the same.

Was it blind luck that you met your significant other? Is it pure chance that your children develop the strongest qualities of both parents? God knows how to put the cogs in place to fulfill His greater purpose. This is how He builds His team. Just as Jethro told Moses, we are to fill an intermediary role of leading our family and friends, while the biggest matters are left in the hands of God. How strong do you want your team to be? It is true that we become who we associate with; therefore, providing our children and our friends with a stabilizing influence and a good moral code of conduct is how we can oversee the success of our little portion of the "department."

As we come to the role of supervision in our personal relationships, it is easy to make the mistake of believing "supervisor" and "parent" are synonymous terms. To become a parent requires nothing more than an act of carnal knowledge, and being a parent in title does not necessarily mean that the supervisor role has been fulfilled. It is tiring to see juvenile halls packed to capacity with young people who have already made their adult lives even more difficult than they should be owing to failed leadership in their home. The parenting role is even more important than the role of department supervisor in a business, because these "employees" are your flesh and blood, and your responsibility.

Why is it so difficult to be supervisors in our own households? Most often it is because we do not realize the role of leadership is not confined to the professional world but has a bigger, longer-lasting impact in our personal lives. To supervise our families requires nothing more than the principles outlined above. Our greatest responsibility is to teach our youth in order that these good traits can be passed from generation to generation, enabling them to be successful adults, good citizens, and God-fearing servants. As every adult was once a child, it is imperative that we pass on one primary lesson: "Obey those who rule over you, and be submissive, for they watch out for your souls, as those who must give account. Let them do so with joy and not with grief, for that would be unprofitable for you" (Hebrews 13:17). What the author of Hebrews is telling us is that we must respect those over us, as they are charged with our welfare, and our duty is to make their job enjoyable. As we grow in leadership roles, we must teach this lesson to those under us, for our accountability to God lies in how we supervise.

# CONCLUSION

Most writings pertaining to leadership focus their attention on a specific discipline or on specific positions. The role of leadership should not be pigeonholed to business managers, military officers, or pastors charged with overseeing a congregation. What makes the qualities of a good leader special is that they can apply to everyone. If we grow up believing only select people can be leaders, how can we ever find our own potential? Some people believe that being a leader is a trait that you are born with, but that viewpoint is a slight to our individual ability to learn and achieve greatness.

Leadership can be taught, but it is up to the individual to want to be more than he may currently be. The saying "Birds of a feather flock together" is definitely accurate. If you do not believe in your own potential to be more than what you are, stop for a second and look at those surrounding you. Do the people around you desire to be more than what they are, or are they content just getting by? What has always made the United States of America a great country is equal opportunity. Somewhere along the way, that viewpoint was drastically skewed until we ultimately found ourselves in a divided culture where equal rewards are desired for unequal work. If equal rewards are not available, a plethora of terms are bandied about until someone gives in to the politically correct mindset. In a system of equal rewards, what motivation is there for the cream to rise to the top? How can a leader evolve in a system where everyone reaps the same harvest? These are difficult times we are living in.

Undoubtedly there are some who saw the title *Secular and Theological Principles* and automatically moved on because of the word "theological." That is a real shame, as they miss a very real connection. There are also those who have probably read through these pages and said to themselves, "I would have added this and this" or "I would have added more technical evolutions to the principles." That was not entirely the goal, or the idea, of putting this together. It is always amazing how many people claim to be atheists or agnostics yet hold strongly conservative values. It is not a coincidence that conservative values find a home in the Christian faith.

The goal of this project was to not only teach someone how to be more successful by being more effective in his professional life but also to bring awareness to the fact that these simple principles can, and should, be applied in everyday life. It is also not a coincidence that the same principles that can make one successful in business and in his personal life are reflected in biblical examples. Some of the greatest stories young people learn in Sunday school are packed with principles of leadership. From Noah and Abraham to John and Paul, and specifically the life of Jesus, examples are set forth for us to follow. They are not just stories of faith but also stories of leadership that have been handed down for thousands of years. Why do we overlook them?

One does not necessarily need to be a Christian to invoke these principles of leadership, because God has blessed us with free will. We are individuals who are free to choose what and whom to believe, and it makes no difference if you choose to not believe in God, because He believes in you and wishes to have a fulfilling relationship with you, but it is your choice. Is it really randomness that makes simple common-sense principles that can bring an enormous amount of success to a person's life, both personally and professionally—the same as what can be found in scripture? God is the Creator, and the Father, and if we view God as a parent, doesn't it make sense that He would give us all the tools we need to be successful? Wouldn't you do the same for your children? "For God so loved the world that he gave His only begotten Son, that whoever believes in Him should not perish but have everlasting life. For God did not send his Son into the world to condemn the world, but that the world through Him might be saved. He who believes in Him is not condemned; but he who does not believe is condemned already, because he has not believed in the name of the only begotten Son of God" (John 3:16–18).

This is *leadership*.

# BIBLIOGRAPHY

Ambrose, Stephen E. *Band of Brothers: E. Company, 506th Regiment, 101st Airborne, From Normandy to Hitler's Eagle's Nest*. New York: Simon & Schuster, 1992.

Business Dictionary. *Peter Principle*. www.businessdictionary.com/ definition. Accessed January 13, 2016

Dalla, Nolan. *"The Difference Between Faith and Trust."* NolanDalla.com. May 19, 2014. http://www.nolandalla. com//?s=trust+and+faith&x=0&y=0.

Howell, Elizabeth. *"How Long Have Humans Been on Earth?"* Universe Today. January 19, 2015. http://www.universetoday. com/38125/how-long-have-humans-been-on-earth/.

# ACKNOWLEDGMENTS

A very special thanks to all those who helped make this project possible either through their contributions, motivations, or belief: my parents, Randy and Carolyn; Keith Miller; Lona Plett; Lisa Swigert; Shannon Savage; Lori Herman; Kenn Holmes; Rodney Patton; Jim Erwin; Dale Comstock; Dr. Gene Jeffries; Robert Fanning; Gary Yackey; Levi Gladman; and Mark Gepfert. Most importantly, I thank Jesus Christ for His grace and mercy. Through Him all things are possible.

# ABOUT THE AUTHOR

Troy Zehnder is a graduate of American Military University, with a BA in homeland security, and Liberty University Baptist Theological Seminary, with an MA in theological studies. He is a member of the International Association of Emergency Managers, the US Naval Institute, and the Civil Air Patrol, and is president of Stone Tiger Consulting (stonetigerllc.com).

Printed in the United States
By Bookmasters